Recuerdos de los Viejitos
Tales of the Río Puerco

Recuerdos de los Viejitos
Tales of the Río Puerco

Collected and Edited by
Nasario García

Portraits by
Isabel A. Rodríguez

Published in cooperation with the
Historical Society of New Mexico

University of New Mexico Press
Albuquerque

Design: Milenda Nan Ok Lee

Library of Congress Cataloging-in-Publication Data

Recuerdos de los viejitos = Tales of the Río Puerco / collected and
edited by Nasario García ; portraits by Isabel A. Rodríguez.
  p. cm.
English and Spanish.
"Published in cooperation with the Historical Society of New
Mexico."
  ISBN 0-8263-1020-6. ISBN 0-8263-1021-4 (pbk.)
  1. Mexican Americans—Puerco River Valley (N.M. and Ariz.)—Social
life and customs.   2. Puerco River Valley (N.M. and Ariz.)—Social
life and customs.   3. New Mexico—Social life and customs.
I. García, Nasario.   II. Rodríguez, Isabel A.   III. Title: Tales of
the Río Puerco.
F805.M5R43   1987
978.9'—dc19   87-20283
                                                                   CIP

Acknowledgments

A sincere debt of gratitude in seeing *Recuerdos de los viejitos* brought to fruition is in order on several fronts. The research fellowship that the Southern Fellowship Fund, an agency of the Council of Southern Universities, Inc., awarded me was extremely helpful in the collection and transcription of some of the stories. The mini grants and dauntless support rendered by James E. Sublette, Director of Research and Graduate Studies, University of Southern Colorado, is greatly appreciated. Mary Sublette's watchful suggestions in organizing the manuscript, particularly the chapter introductions, cannot be easily forgotten. Scheduling photograph sessions and setting up interviews was a time-consuming endeavor; accordingly, I am grateful to my sisters Elsie Gallegos and Julia Jaramillo, who reside in Albuquerque, for their generous devotion of time and energy toward those aims. I would also like to extend my heartfelt thanks to Myra Ellen Jenkins, Spencer Wilson, and John P. Conron, Publications Committee, Historical Society of New Mexico, for their unstinted interest in and support of my project. Lastly, a very special recognition goes to Elizabeth A. Reyes, The University of New Mexico, for her staunch appreciation of New Mexico's *hispano* folklore, and to Barbara Guth, Editorial Assistant, The University of New Mexico, whose critical eye helped improve the quality of the manuscript.

Dedication

*To my beloved mother,
Agapita López-García,
Que Dios la tenga en la gloria.*

Contents

Chapter 2: Their Tragedies

Contents   xi

Chapter 5: The Supernatural

Foreword

In Colonial New Mexico during the 1760s, several land-poor residents, most of them from the Río Grande Valley settlements around Albuquerque, petitioned the governor for large grants of farming, and especially of grazing, lands in the valley of the Río Puerco of the east and its bordering grasslands and high mesas. They established ranchos on their concessions and their stock increased because of the excellent pasturage. Their holdings were on the fringe of Navajo country, however, and the valley floor provided a convenient and accessible route for Navajo war parties bent on raiding the Río Grande plazas and Indian Pueblos. Along the way, they struck the ranchos and ran off the livestock. The formidable mesas provided refuge for the raiders on their return when too closely pursued by avenging military and settler forces.

So effective were these attacks that periodically the Río Puerco families, gathering up any surviving stock, abandoned their new homes for the comparative safety of numbers in their former places of residence. Confrontation with the Navajo would then temporarily abate, and the hardy stockmen would return to their ranchos, only to suffer another attack, and the disheartening cycle of abandonment would be repeated. The grants were largely deserted when the United

States occupied New Mexico in 1846. Late in the century the large acreages claimed for them came into the hands of Anglo speculators.

In the meantime, after the establishment of a reservation for the Navajos in 1868, following their unhappy incarceration at the Bosque Redondo, land-poor families from the Río Grande Valley region again moved into the silt-laden central valley of the Río Puerco west of the Jémez Pueblo. Within a twenty-mile distance they founded four small settlements, in each of which they built their houses and a small church within the traditional village pattern. They also brought with them their one hundred and fifty year-old farming-pastoral way of life, as well as their religious faith and beliefs, and the attitudes and folkways out of which a dynamic New Mexico Hispanic culture had been formed during that long period.

For a time the villagers prospered, in a modest sort of way, or at least were able to support themselves and their extended families. Gradually, however, the forces of nature and man's depletion of the fragile Río Puerco Valley environment forced these pioneers again to abandon their homes, their fields, and even their grazing lands, and to return once more to the Albuquerque area.

Little has been written concerning this period and area of settlement. The factual history of one village has been ably documented by Jack D. Rittenhouse in *Cabezón, a New Mexico Ghost Town*, published in 1965. Even this excellent work, however, lacks the flavor of primary accounts by those who actually lived there, for the simple reason that those accounts were unrecorded. This study records some primary accounts as told by those who lived in the villages of Casa Salazar, Guadalupe, Cabezón and San Luis, or to whom the accounts were told by those who had lived there. When the people came back to the Albuquerque area they brought with them the oral histories of events which had taken place in their Río Puerco homeland, their own reminiscences of personal experiences and religious manifestations, as well as the legends and other folklore which had grown up around the isolated communities. Throughout these accounts, however, the basic attitudes, beliefs and values of the society which they had taken with them in the first place were still discernible. Fortunately, this body of vibrant oral history and literature from a previously unrecorded area can now further enrich the age-old cultural heritage of Hispanic New Mexico.

But, *Recuerdos de los viejitos* have another and very special significance. As the author points out, language is the basic ingredient of a culture. Thanks to its bilingual format this study particularly illustrates the continuity and vitality of the Spanish vernacular still spoken by New Mexicans, particularly by those from backgrounds in outlying rural areas, including the persistence of archaisms from the colonial period. The language of the narrators is usually straightforward and matter of fact, frequently humorous, often tender and sometimes downright earthy.

Above all, the stories make good reading in themselves. There is even an intriguing account of a UFO sighting in the Río Puerco Valley, a much better tale, to be sure, than most of those already in print. *Recuerdos de los Viejitos/Tales of the Río Puerco* is the fifteenth volume in the series copublished by the University of New Mexico Press and the Historical Society of New Mexico.

Myra Ellen Jenkins
Santa Fe, New Mexico

Recuerdos de los Viejitos
Tales of the Río Puerco

Introduction

Recuerdos de los viejitos/Tales of the Río Puerco is testimony to an assortment of experiences among Hispanos who once resided in the villages, today ghost towns, of San Luis (La Tijera), Cabezón (La Posta), Guadalupe (Ojo del Padre) and Casa Salazar, in the Río Puerco Valley in west-central New Mexico (Map I). The stories and vignettes offer, among other things, an insight into the virtues and foibles, beliefs and tragedies which culminate in the portrayal of Hispanic heritage in the Río Puerco Valley. Moreover, the narratives will enable the reader to learn firsthand how ordinary people speak and relate experiences, some with more perspicacity than others, of course. In brief, *Recuerdos de los viejitos* contains a corpus of literature that hitherto has been unavailable to the reading public.

Accordingly, it is hoped that this collection of stories by former villagers from the Río Puerco Valley who were born and/or lived there will contribute, if not in filling a lacuna in oral literature of New Mexico, at least in representing a geographical area different from the traditional northern part of the state or the Río Grande Valley. To my knowledge only casual references exist in such literature of the Río Puerco Valley. Charles F. Lummis in *The Land of Poco Tiempo* talks about "La Calandria," a folk song heard in Los Cerros Cuates (The

Twin Peaks) between Cabezón and Guadalupe. Salomón Lovato, one of the narrators in *Recuerdos de los viejitos,* also referred to "La Calandria" in our interview. Marc Simmons in *Taos to Tomé: True Tales of Hispanic New Mexico* places two of his stories in Cebolleta, farther south from either of the villages mentioned above, but within the Río Puerco area nonetheless. Stanley L. Robe in *Hispanic Legends from New Mexico,* which contains hundreds of entries, includes but one short tale from the Río Puerco Valley.

The west-central portion of the Río Puerco Valley lies about forty miles, "as the crow flies," northwest of Albuquerque; by car one must travel about sixty miles just to reach San Luis, the first of the four villages, located a few miles from Highway 44 between Bernalillo and Cuba. The Río Puerco (Dirty or Muddy River), from which the valley derives its name, is a tributary of the Río Grande. It rises south of Cuba, within the Nacimiento Mountains in Sandoval County, and meanders through the Río Puerco Valley along San Luis, Cabezón, Guadalupe and Casa Salazar, finally emptying into the Río Grande about forty-five miles south of Albuquerque.

The topography of the Río Puerco Valley is contradictory, providing austere but at the same time beautiful sites. From San Luis to Casa Salazar, the last of the villages of interest to us, is approximately twenty miles. The terrain within this area, as one follows the contour of the Río Puerco, consists of lava-capped mesas, buttes, deep-gutted arroyos, many of which empty into the Río Puerco, plus cañadas, broken sandstone and volcanic peaks or plugs that possess a certain majestic beauty as they loom in the horizon.

Of the many volcanic peaks in the region, the one that has attracted the most attention over the years is El Cerro Cabezón (The Big-Headed Peak), the most spectacular and menacing, rising about 8,000 feet in altitude and, lying south

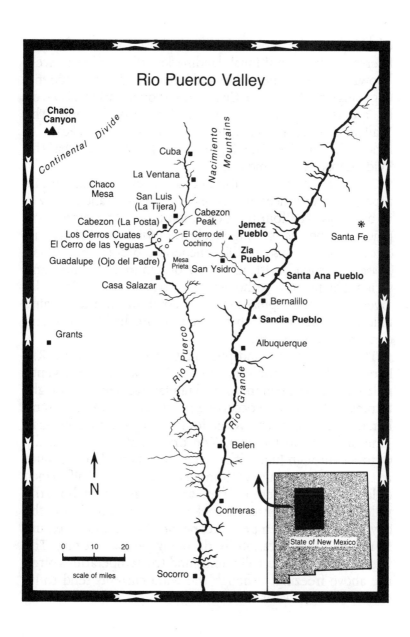

Rio Puerco Valley

Chaco Canyon

Continental Divide

Nacimiento Mountains

Cuba

La Ventana

Chaco Mesa

San Luis (La Tijera)

Cabezon Peak

Cabezon (La Posta)

Los Cerros Cuates

El Cerro de las Yeguas

El Cerro del Cochino

Jemez Pueblo

Zia Pueblo

Guadalupe (Ojo del Padre)

Mesa Prieta

San Ysidro

Santa Fe

Santa Ana Pueblo

Casa Salazar

Bernalillo

Sandia Pueblo

Grants

Rio Puerco

Rio Grande

Albuquerque

N

Belen

Contreras

State of New Mexico

0   10   20

scale of miles

Socorro

of Cabezón, the most celebrated ghost town in the Río Puerco Valley. Additional landmarks, albeit not as well-known, except to the natives and history students or students of geology, are Los Cerros Cuates, mentioned earlier, El Ojo de las Yeguas (The Mares' Spring), El Arroyo de la Tapia (The Walled Arroyo), El Cerro del Cochino (The Hog's Peak), El Rincón del Cochino (The Hog's Corner), La Cañada Ancha (The Wide Cañada), to name a few.

The vegetation of the Río Puerco Valley, coupled with its topography, enhances the region's scenic beauty and quality in its own way. The four most common types of vegetation are piñon, juniper (*sabino*), big sagebrush (*chamiso*) and shortgrass (*sacate*). One can also readily encounter broom snakewood (*escoba de la víbora*), with its yellow bloom in late winter and spring. This plant, together with the cocklebur (*cadillo*) and the silver-like donkey spinach (*quelite de burro*), add to the terrain's unique character, but these last two are highly toxic and dangerous to livestock.

The temperatures and precipitation of the semi-arid Río Puerco Valley do not vary dramatically within the twenty mile range of the region. Annual rainfall averages about eight to nine inches, mostly occurring in July, August, and September. It is not unusual, however, for the rainy season to begin in June and end in October. The dry months are generally October through June, although winter snowfalls contribute to the valley's moisture with an average of about a half an inch or less per month. Temperatures are constant throughout the valley. Summer months are cool at night and hot during the day, with daytime temperatures ranging in the 80s and 90s, and in the evenings occasionally dropping below freezing. The winter months are usually sunny and the temperatures often rise above freezing, although the wind currents tend to increase the chill factor in the valley.

The settlement of the Río Puerco Valley began in Navajo country in the 1760s with the approval of several grazing grants by Governor Tomás Vélez Cachupín. Nevertheless, for approximately one hundred years settlements were topsy-turvy at best due to repeated Indian raids on the settlers' ranches. A resumption of a tranquil existence along the Río Puerco, after the establishment of the Navajo reservation, resulted in permanent Hispanic settlements (Map I). Settlers began to return, for example, to Casa Salazar, Cabezón, and Guadalupe in the 1860s and 1870s. The three Hispanic villages alluded to here, and San Luis as well, prospered for a time (in their own right), attracting "foreigners" as traders and merchants and served by stage and freight lines. But a population decline beginning after World War I worsened during the Great Depression and World War II. By 1958, the last school, as well as the post office and grocery store in Guadalupe, both operated by Adelita Gonzales and her kin, closed. This family, too, moved to Albuquerque, where the majority of the villagers who once resided in the Río Puerco Valley now live.

The people who migrated to the Río Puerco Valley in the eighteenth and nineteenth centuries did so in the hope of improving their lot rather than staying in heavily populated Río Grande Valley settlements like Albuquerque, Bernalillo, Algodones, Alameda, Los Ranchos de Albuquerque and Atrisco. Later, people even went from Antón Chico on the Pecos River. However, the majority of the people whose stories appear in *Recuerdos de los viejitos* were born in the Río Puerco Valley and lived there until moving back to the Río Grande Valley where most of their forefathers had first settled. These inhabitants living in the cluster of Hispanic villages, earned a modest living as farmers or ranchers; some tried their hand at both. Homesteaded land was farmed and passed on to the children. Until the 1930s ranchers raised their animals, primarily cattle and sheep, in the "wide-open" spaces without any land restrictions until a government's concern for soil erosion compelled it to impose restrictions on land use to avoid further deterioration of the soil. Some stories in *Recuerdos de los viejitos* attest to the bitterness and resentment of the villagers toward the government for what was felt to be its cruelty and ruthlessness in dealing with the issue of land use. Protecting the environment became a primary concern to the government; safeguarding the survival of the remaining animals, however, appeared to the local people to be of secondary importance.

People eventually found themselves at the mercy of the forces of nature. With progressive effects of drought and soil erosion life became more difficult for villagers dependent on farming or ranching. Water was a most treasured commodity and, if it did not rain, the makeshift reservoirs or dams which stored water for irrigating became useless. Often the dams would rupture during a downpour. Then farmers, whose farmland was not adjacent to the acequia system, did not benefit from irrigation and had to rely solely on rain and run-off (*de temporal*) from the cañadas for their crops to grow. Flash floods due to torrential rains often resulted in uprooting less hearty crops such as pinto beans, a staple in the community, or ruining others.

Today a large percentage of the people still own property and some are frequent weekend visitors to the village where they used to live. Others who are retired extend their visitations to repair the old home, rest, and no doubt to reminisce about the past. San Luis, unlike Cabezón, Guadalupe and Casa Salazar, continues to be inhabited by two or three families. Together with those former residents who return on occasion they continue to maintain the church, and Mass is celebrated there periodically. During the last several years, particularly, those who once belonged to the Penitente Brothers have reenacted in San Luis the march to Mount Calvary and Christ's crucifixion on Good Friday. Guadalupe, Cabezón and Casa Salazar have not been as fortunate. Vandals have ransacked people's homes, destroyed their churches, desecrated the cemeteries, and, in a few instances, slaughtered livestock.

In 1977 I undertook an oral history project concerning the people of the four Río Puerco Valley villages. Subsequently, the emphasis was shifted to include only Guadalupe, the village where I spent my childhood, and where my family has owned property for over one hundred years. Meantime, it became apparent that each interview conducted with former residents of the Río Puerco Valley contained several stories (*historias*) of interest. These stories were either based on the narrators' personal experiences, or they had been transmitted orally to them by someone in their family. This enticed me to return to some of the interviewees and to seek others, for more stories. The choice as to whom to reinterview was strictly an eclectic one, that is, on the basis of their story-telling ability and interests.

Of the fifteen contributors to *Recuerdos de los viejitos*, only four are women. One of these is my paternal grandmother who was interviewed in 1968 before she died. Additional women, as well as men, were interviewed, but since they knew few oral stories they are not included. A possible explanation for more men having stories to tell than women is because of women being isolated at home, while the men enjoyed more freedom in their daily lives.

The interviewees, many of whom I knew as a child, and some of whom have died since the interviews, range in age from fifty-eight to ninety-three years. Except for one individual who recounted his stories in English, Edumenio Lovato, the remainder of the contributors did so in Spanish, their native language. The majority of them had little education. One of the female interviewees never attended school. Education was deemed to be for men only, and even that was usually limited to completing a third or, sometimes an eighth grade education. Nevertheless, most of interviewees learned to read and write in Spanish of their own accord at home; a few even learned English as adults after they abandoned their village and moved to places like Albuquerque. Today, however, some still speak only Spanish.

The manner (narrative style) in which stories were told varied, depending on the narrator's background and personality, his or her ability to recount tales, and the subject at hand. The topic tended to set the tone for the story which ranged from the emotional to the light-hearted, from the realistic to the tragic. The content, as well as the language of the narratives, was predicated upon one or all of the foregoing components.

Language provides the linkage between people and their culture. Implicit in this partnership are cultural values that reflect the spirit of a people, namely their attitudes, prejudices, beliefs, humor, inspirations, delusions, and human frailties. In conveying any of these characteristics, language plays a vital role because each sound, word, or expression commands a certain amount of attention. This is particularly true of the people who contributed to *Recuerdos de los viejitos*.

The language found in *Recuerdos de los viejitos* is not very diverse. All contributors employed standard Spanish with a smattering of archaisms (*mesmo-mismo*), regionalisms (*golver-volver*), Anglicism (*chanza-oportunidad*), idiomatic expressions, and the like. In some cases a narrator was apt to employ in the context of a story two or even three different pronunciations of the same word (e.g., *pos, pus, pues*). There was, quite naturally, a propensity for repeating pause words or expressions that constituted an integral part of the narrator's lexicon. Repetition resulted either in creating monotony or incoherency or both within the internal structure of a narrative. While *Recuerdos de los viejitos* is an attempt at sharing oral literature and not a study on dialectology, it is important to remember that manner of speech reflects not only an environment but language realism; e.g., its earthiness as well.

In transcribing the stories for *Recuerdos de los viejitos* a conscious effort was made to uphold the integrity of the language. Orthography, for the most part, reflects pronunciation. Only in isolated cases (e.g., *b-v*) was the standard or modern spelling invoked. However, changes in syntax or deletions were part of the editing process so as to enhance the narrative quality and thus avoid inconsistencies, cacophony, and *non sequiturs*. Making the stories as readable as possible whenever necessary was an utmost consideration.

A similar approach and attitude were adopted in the translation; of primary concern was not the basic translation *per se* but the conveying of the thoughts and the manner in which they flowed. Thus, there were situations in which the meaning or intent of a word, phrase or expression took precedence over literal translation. This was done to sustain the spirit of the story while at the same time doing justice to content as well as the mode of story-telling.

The stories expose the reader to a form of oral literature which reflects the personal experiences of the inhabitants of the Río Puerco Valley in west-central New Mexico. A projection of the villagers' daily lives and existence in an environment imbued with their cultural heritage is tempered by a blending of stoicism and personal pride. All of this culminated both singularly and collectively in the molding of their character and individual identity.

The text is organized in a bilingual (Spanish/English) format.

Each chapter centers around a theme ranging from the people themselves to the supernatural. The stories contained therein reflect that particular focus.

A brief biographical sketch in English of each contributor appears in alphabetical order at the end of the text in an attempt to highlight certain traits or attributes that (s)he possesses which indeed may be reflected in the contents of their stories.

Regional or local terms that appear in the narratives will be highlighted under *Glossary* with the modern or standard spelling next to them. The person who reads the stories in Spanish will thus be able to distinguish between the local and more universal usage of words. At the same time, the Spanish speaker or linguist can appreciate the discrepancy in the pronunciation of the same word within the Río Puerco Valley region and elsewhere. Finally, the reader will be able to detect words whose archaic pronunciation has survived for over four hundred years since the *conquistadores* visited New Mexico in the sixteenth century.

1

The People

The Hispanos who lived in the Río Puerco Valley were shaped by their environment–the Indians, the river, the strangers, particularly the non-Hispanics, who came to the villages from surrounding areas, the land, and the animals from which they drew a large part of their livelihood. In the earlier years, as can be seen from the first three stories, the Indians were one of the most disrupting factors in their lives. Though "Rafael Lovato and the Pawnee Indians" actually occurred near Las Vegas, New Mexico, the kidnapped boy was related to the family of Edumenio Lovato, who lived in San Luis. "Peddlers," "The Late Sotero," and the later "Stealing the Church Bell," give a vivid illustration of the distrust that was prevalent toward outsiders who came into the villages, while "Even the Dead Voted," shows a tolerant cynicism to the realities of life.

In the 1930s, conservationists became aware that the range lands ranchers rented from the federal government were being badly overgrazed. The result of this overgrazing, was a significant loss of top soil and the cutting of deep arroyos. To stop the destruction, Congress passed the Taylor Grazing Act in 1934. The act decreed that the size of the herds must be cut. While the law was necessary to prevent further deterioration of the land, it was a traumatic experience for the men and women who saw their healthy cattle destroyed, and they were deeply bitter toward the government agents who enforced the law. "We Were Humiliated" depicts the depth of the anger and the helplessness that the ranchers on the Río Puerco felt at their inability to prevent the destruction of the animals that were such an important part of their lives.

Particularly in the early years, horsemanship was much admired in the Río Puerco Valley, as is revealed in "Good Cowboys," and again in "Eduardo Baca." Eduardo Baca was respected, also, as a latter-day Robin Hood who took from the rich but helped the poor. His daring appealed to the poor people, and, while some of the men might ride with a posse, few would have given information about him to the law.

The stories and vignettes in this first chapter give impressions of life as it was then, as told to me by the people who lived it. Injected into each tale is the personality of each of the storytellers, as well as a scene from a unique way of life that is now gone.

La navajocería

Juan Armijo

Yo me acuerdo que llegaron a llegar hasta en casa los llorones que iban. ¡Quién sabe de dónde vendrían! Como la plebe no entendía, iban a meter miedo allá estos llorones. "La Llorona," dicían, porque traiba una sábana y un palo. "Uh, uh, uh, uh," hacía y entre más largo el ruido, más miedo nos daba, ¿ves? Y arrancábanos todos a volar.

Tamién nosotros, con la plebe en casa, salimos a escaparnos, dos veces, porque jueron los navajoses, que llegaban en la noche cuando se hacía oscuro. Estaba mi mamá sola con nosotros; estábanos medianos. En lo oscuro nos juimos. Tuvimos que, que pescar el río, todo el Río Puerco pa bajo, pa que no nos vieran los indios, pa que saliéranos a juir de ellos. Se aproximaba en las casas la navajocería, como era guerra más antes todo eso de ai del Río Puerco. Y estaban aquellos navajoses que no los podía cortar el gobierno.

Güeno. Yo les brincaba a los navajoses. Yo estaba chiquito pero era el más valiente. Yo salía atrás de ellos. Pus yo era muy atroz. Yo no les tenía miedo a los navajoses. Tenía un rifle 410 de aquellos grandototes, de los que había antes. ¡Unos cartuchotes de este pelo! Le temblaban los navajoses a los cartuchos. ¡Pam! Caiba yo boca arriba; me aventaba el rifle. Vían el lumbregón de aquel rifle y aquí iba la navajocería a volar.

The Whole Navajo Clan

Juan Armijo

I remember that even the so-called wailing men or women got to stop at our house. Who knows where they came from! Since the children didn't know any better, these wailing men or women would go to our village to scare the dickens out of them. "It's The Wailing Woman," people proclaimed, because she had on a bedsheet and carried a stick. She went "Uh, uh, uh, uh," and the more prolonged the noise, the more frightened we became. Got it? And we'd all take off running.

Also, we, along with the rest of the children at home, twice had to leave in order to escape from the Navajos who would show up at night when it got dark. My mom was alone with us; we were little. We took off in the dark. We had to, to catch the river, the Río Puerco, and head downstream, so that the Indians couldn't see us, so we could flee from them. The whole Navajo clan, being that they were at war all along the Río Puerco, they'd come close to the homes. And those Navajos were such that not even the government was capable of restraining them.

Very well. I'd jump on the Navajos. I was very small. I'd go after them. But then I was also very much of a cutup. I wasn't afraid of the Navajos. I had one of those great big 410 shotguns (single shot shotgun), like the ones they used to have long ago. Huge bullets, this big! The Navajos trembled at the sight of those huge shells. Pam! I'd land flat on my back; the rifle would knock me down. They'd see the big blast from that rifle and here you'd have the whole Navajo clan off-and-running.

Los navajoses

Emilia Padilla-García

Los navajoses mataron a mi agüelo, ai en Las Cejitas Blancas, en La Ceja, yendo pa en casa, pa Gualupe. Mi agüelo se llamaba Luis, Luis Tafoya. Era su papá de mi mamá. Ai en Las Cejitas Blancas, ai lo mataron los navajoses. Él vivía aquí en Corrales, y éstos vinieron hacer mal aquí en Corrales. Y salió mi papá grande, y salieron otras gentes, y a mi agüelo y a dos más de ai de Corrales los mataron. Resulta que jue un cuerpo de navajoses a la placita de Corrales. Entraron en la noche. Entraron a robar. Y, eh, eh, tenía la gente antes carne de cecinas hechas, o comida en lugares donde consideraba que los navajoses no podían entrar, pero éstos entraban.

Cuando mataron a mi papá grande no estaría yo nacida, pero él tenía una mula que le llamaba La Mula de Estima. Estaba medio rico; no estaba muy mal. Y en este trascorral tenía esa mula y una porción de carne, en una reata de cuero que le decían, de cuero de vaca. Y se llevaron, y se llevaron la mula. Así no sé cómo salió mi papá grande en pues de los navajoses que traiban flechas. Con eso peleaban los navajoses, con la flecha. Ya a ellos, a mi papá grande y a los otros dos, cuando llegó, me platicaba a mí mi mamá grande, cuando ya estuve más grande, cuando llegó el auxilio, ya a ellos los habían matao. Y toavía mataron dos navajoses.

Un hermano cuñao de mi agüelo, me decía mi mamá grande a mí, se quedó con un navajó así de las greñas muerto él, y muerto el navajó. Mi tío, su hermanito de mi agüelo, era el otro. Eso me platicaba a mí mi mamá grande. Ésa jue la que duró más viva después, que yo ya alcancé a platicar poquito con ella. Estaba medianita yo.

Se quedó con un navajó, creo, de las greñas, este hermano cuñao de mi agüelo. Y los otros navajoses salieron a juir. Ya cuando la ayuda llegó—la remuda—ya los habían matao a mi agüelo y a los otros dos. Y es que eran hombres muy útiles, este mi agüelo y su hermano cuñao. ¡Muy útiles!

Pero estaban en guerra los navajoses; estaban en guerra. Ai onde vivíanos nosotros en Gualupe, ai estaban ellos. De ai estaban viniendo a pelear y bajaban a Corrales de noche, creo. Todo eso pasó antes de que nosotros naciéramos, quizás. Cuando estaban toavía mis agüelos vivos.

The Navajos

Emilia Padilla-Garcia

The Navajos killed my grandfather. They did so there in Las Cejitas Blancas (The Tiny White Summits), in La Ceja, on the way home, toward Guadalupe. My grandfather's name was Luis, Luis Tafoya. He was my maternal grandfather. It was right there in Las Cejitas Blancas, that's where the Navajos murdered him. He lived here in Corrales, and the Navajos came to cause destruction. My grandpa went out to see what was going on, as did others, and my grandfather, plus two others, were killed there in Corrales.

As it turned out, it was a cadre of Navajos that went to the small village of Corrales. It was night time. They went to steal. And, uh, people long ago used to have strips of jerky or other food in places where they thought the Navajos could not enter, but they used to just the same.

When my grandpa was killed I probably wasn't even born yet, but, in any case, he had a mule called La Mula de Estima (The Mule of Esteem). He was a little rich; not bad off. And in this back court he kept that mule and a portion of meat, strung on what they called a riata made of hide, cowhide. And the Navajos stole, they stole the mule. Consequently, I don't know how it was that my grandpa was able to go after the Navajos who were carrying bows and arrows. That's what they fought with. As for my grandpa and the other two men, my grandma would tell me, when I was a little older, that when help arrived, all three already had been murdered. Still, the three of them were able to kill two Navajos.

A brother-in-law of my grandfather, my grandma would tell me, died holding on to a Navajo by the hair. The Navajo was also dead. My uncle, my grandfather's smaller brother, was the other one who was killed, according to my grandma. She's the one who lived longer after all of this. She's the one I managed to talk with a little about this incident. I was quite small.

As I tell you, this brother-in-law of my grandfather died holding on to a Navajo by the hair. The rest of the Navajos took off running and, when help arrived, my grandfather and the other two men had already been killed. And I understand that they were very capable men. Very capable!

But the Navajos were at war; they were at war. There in Guadalupe where we used to live, that's where they were. From there they'd come down at night to Corrales, I believe, to fight. All of that went on before any of us were born, while my grandparents were still alive, I believe.

Rafael Lovato y los indios Pawnee

Edumenio Lovato

Rafael Lovato y dos otros muchachos, cuyo apellido era Montoya (los dos Montoya no eran parientes), fueron capturados y robados por un grupo de indios Pawnee. Los tres muchachos estaban cuidando borregas en el llano a unas cuantas millas al este de Las Vegas, Nuevo México cuando pasó esto. Rafael tenía trece años y los Montoya también eran de la misma edad en aquel entonces.

Los indios Pawnee, una confederación de cuatro tribus, era gente agricultora que vivía al lado del Río Platte en Nebraska que iba a dar hasta el sur en el estado de Kansas. Las tribus vivían en casas permanentes hechas de madera, o sea, cabañas de troncos, y tierra, usando el *tepee* mayormente cuando iban de caza. Las aldeas o pueblos estaban retirados los unos de los otros.

Los Pawnee y sus prisioneros viajaron muchos días antes de que el grupo de indios llegara al primer establecimiento. Aquí fueron separados los tres muchachos por los indios. A Rafael lo detuvieron en la aldea y a los muchachos Montoya se los llevaron, cada uno a un establecimiento diferente. Al día siguiente, después de que el grupo de indios llegó a la aldea, los indios le agujeraron las orejas a Rafael y le pusieron aros de metal, que le colgaban de la perilla de la oreja, uno de cada oreja. Después de esta experiencia dolorosa, Rafael fue dado por hijo a una pareja india.

Los padres adoptivos de Rafael no tenían hijos, y desde un principio lo trataban con cariño, ansiosos por conseguir su amistad.

Le daban bien de comer, aunque al principio a Rafael no le gustaba mucho la comida, pero disfrutaba del hambre menos y dentro de poco se acostumbró a comer los víveres que le servían. Él se sentía muy triste al verse entre gente desconocida; ni siquiera podía comunicarse con ellos. La bondad de sus padres adoptivos disminuía un tanto su tristeza. Con el tiempo su madre adoptiva le hizo a Rafael su primer par de pantalones de cuero y una chaqueta, y su padre adoptivo le hizo su primer par de tewas. Los dos empezaron a enseñarle la lengua Pawnee.

Según los días se iban convirtiendo en semanas y meses, el joven prisionero se fue acostumbrando a su medio ambiente nuevo, la gente y su modo de vivir. Él se esforzó por ayudar, porque todos en la aldea hacían lo que les tocaba de trabajo. Dentro de poco Rafael demostró en ser digno de sus aprehensores. Poco a poco aprendió el idioma Pawnee, el poder comunicar su vida con la gente se hizo más soportable, más cómoda. Empezó a hacerse amigo de muchachos de su edad. Los acompañaba en viajes de caza menor. Aunque Rafael se puso menos triste, nunca dejó de pensar en su familia, su hogar, y sus dos amigos, los Montoya. Esperaba que a sus dos amigos les estuviera yendo bien como a él.

Con el tiempo sus aprehensores le enseñaron a Rafael el uso del arco y la flecha, el arte de cazar, y cazar al acecho animales silvestres. Aprendió a pasearse en sus caballos entrenados que usaban para cazar bufalós silvestres. El bufaló era el abastecimiento principal de carne de los indios. Rafael observó que esta gente utilizaba el animal entero: la carne para comida, el cuero para *tepees*, equipaje, cabrestos y hasta para algunas de sus ropas. De manera que el cazar de la bestia silvestre era un oficio importante de los cazadores indios. Era un oficio duro y peligroso. Solamente los cazadores bien entrenados y con experiencia participaban en el verdadero perseguir y matar del bufaló silvestre. Rafael era muy joven y carecía de experiencia para tomar parte en este trabajo. Sin embargo, sí acompañaba a los cazadores en excursiones de bufaló para ayudarles preparar el armazón para transportarlo al establecimiento.

Durante los cinco años de prisión Rafael aprendió muchas cosas de sus aprehensores. Aprendió la lengua Pawnee bien. Aprendió de la vida de los indios Pawnee: sus costumbres, su comportamiento y la relación existente entre unos y los otros; y, sus creencias. El observó muchos de sus ritos extraños y ceremonias religiosas, y aprendió algo de lo que ellos representaban.

Por lo visto, Rafael no apreciaba la idea de tener que pasar el resto de su vida entre sus aprehensores. El pensar en escaparse de este ambiente inaceptable debe haberle torturado con frecuencia, porque un día tuvo la oportunidad de escaparse y lo intentó.

Durante un viaje de caza a muchas millas de la aldea, Rafael tuvo la primera oportunidad de escaparse de sus aprehensores. Se escabulló del partido de caza, y huyó sin saber a dónde iba. Fue un atentado atrevido, porque bien sabía que tomaría muchos días para llegar a su casa, y no estaba preparado para el largo viaje. Además, no sabía en qué dirección quedaba su casa. Por días se anduvo por el campo hasta que al fin se dio cuenta que andaba perdido sin esperanza. Entonces decidió que no tenía más remedio que regresar al establecimiento de los indios. Rafael había fracasado en su primer atentado de escape.

De regreso a la aldea Rafael mató un venado. Por lo menos no volvería con las manos vacías; eso pensó él. Tenía intenciones de llevar el armazón del venado a sus padres adoptivos. Según iba entrando poco a poco en el establecimeinto hacia la cabaña de troncos de sus padres adoptivos, un grupo de cazadores indios, lo siguieron a Rafael y lo rodearon, y antes de que tuviera tiempo de apearse de su caballo, dos de sus aprehensores lo agarraron y bruscamente lo bajaron de su montura. Los indios enfadados demandaron saber por qué había tratado de huirse. Rafael les dijo que se había perdido. Los indios aceptaron su explicación y lo dejaron ir. Aunque Rafael había fracasado en su primer atentado de libertad, ya había decidido tratar de hacerlo de nuevo. Rafael nunca tuvo esa oportunidad porque fue rescatado.

Durante sus cinco años de prisión, Rafael había vivido una vida diferente: la vida de los indios Pawnee. No le gustó. Prefería la libertad, su familia, y su casa.

Rafael Lovato And The Pawnee Indians

Edumenio Lovato

Rafael Lovato and two other boys, surnamed Montoya (the two Montoyas were not related), were captured and carried away by a party of Pawnee Indians. The three boys were tending sheep out on the range some miles east of Las Vegas, New Mexico when this happened. Rafael was thirteen years old and the two Montoyas were also in their early teens at the time.

The Pawnee Indians, a confederation of four tribes, were an agricultural people, dwelling along the Platte River in Nebraska and ranging as far south to the state of Kansas. The tribes lived in permanent homes made of logs and earth using the tepee mostly for hunting excursions. The villages or pueblos were separated some distances from each other.

The Pawnees and their captives traveled many days before the party reached the first Indian settlement. Here, the three boys were separated by the Indians. Rafael was kept in the village and the two Montoya boys were taken away, each boy to a different settlement. The following day after the party arrived at the village, the Indians pierced Rafael's ears and metal rings, one on each ear, were placed hanging from each ear lobe. After this painful experience, Rafael was given away for adoption to an Indian couple.

Rafael's foster parents had no children of their own, and from the beginning treated him kindly, eager to win his friendship. They fed him well, though at first Rafael found the food not much to his liking, but he relished hunger less and soon got used to eating the victuals placed before him. He felt very lonely finding himself among strange people, not even being able to communicate with them. The kindness of his foster parents somewhat eased his loneliness. In time his foster mother fashioned for Rafael his first pair of buckskin breeches and jacket, and his new father made for him a pair of moccasins. They began to teach him the Pawnee language.

As the days turned to weeks and months, the young captive became more adapted to his new surroundings, the people and their lives. He made himself useful, for everyone in the village did their share of work. In a short time Rafael won the approval of his captors. Little by little he learned the Pawnee language, and being able to communicate with the people his life became more bearable, more comfortable. He began to make friends with young boys his age. He joined them in their hunting trips for small wild game. Though Rafael became less lonely, he never ceased to think about his family and home, and his two friends, the Montoyas. He hoped his two friends were faring as well as he was.

In time his captors taught Rafael the use of the bow and arrow, and the art of hunting and stalking wild game. He learned to ride their trained horses used in hunting the wild buffalo. The buffalo was the main meat supply of the Indians. Rafael observed that these people utilized the whole animal: the meat for food, the skin for making tepees, baggages, ropes, and even some of their clothing. So hunting the wild beast was an important occupation of the Indian hunters. It was a hard and dangerous occupation. Only well-trained and experienced hunters took part in the actual chasing and killing of the wild buffalo. Rafael was too young and inexperienced to take part in this work. He did, however, join the hunters in buffalo hunting trips to help in preparing the carcasses for transportation to the settlement.

During the five years in captivity Rafael learned many things from his captors. He learned the Pawnee language well. He learned about the life of the Pawnee Indian people: their customs, their behavior and relation to each other, their beliefs. He witnessed many of their strange rituals and religious ceremonies, and learned some of their meaning.

Evidently, Rafael did not cherish the idea of spending the rest of his life among his captors. His thought of escaping from this unacceptable environment must have been on his mind often, for one day he got his first opportunity and tried to escape.

During a hunting trip many miles from the Indian village, Rafael got his first chance to ride away from his captors. He slipped away from the hunting party, and rode off without any sense of direction. It was a daring try, for he well knew it would take many days to reach his home, and he was unprepared for the long trip. Besides, he did not know the direction to his home. For days he wandered over the range until finally he realized he was hopelessly lost. He decided then that his only choice was to ride back to the Indian settlement. Rafael had failed in his first attempt to escape.

On his way back to the village Rafael killed a deer. At least he would not come back empty-handed, he thought. He intended to take the deer carcass to his foster parents. As he slowly rode into the settlement towards his foster parents' cabin, a group of Indian hunters followed and surrounded Rafael, and before he had time to dismount from his horse, a couple of his captors grabbed him and roughly pulled him off his mount. The Indians angrily demanded why he had tried to run away. Rafael told them that he had become separated from the hunting party and had become lost. The Indians accepted his explanation and let him go. Though Rafael had failed in his first attempt at freedom, he had already made up his mind to try again. Rafael never had that chance for he was rescued.

During his five years in captivity, Rafael had lived a different life: the life of the Pawnee Indians. He did not like it. He preferred his freedom, his family, and his home.

Los vendedores

Adrián Chávez

Estos vendedores de aquí del Río—de Alburquerque—que iban a Gualupe, engañaban a la gente muncho. No se vendía nada con seguridá de que juera güena. Y vengamos a hablar de las composturas pa las mujeres: cremas y todo eso. Llegó a haber munchas personas que compraban cualquier pomada, vamos a decir, y loo compraban un bonche de botellitas con diferentes *labels*. A todas les echaban de lo mismo. Te vendían dos, tres botellas pa la piel.

Y otros que trataban de ser dotorcitos, éstos iban aá a curar brujerías, cosas así. Pus ya ellos llevaban todo listo de aquí. Por eso le digo que eso es estudio. Hay píldoras, munchas diferentes clases. Le decían a esta mujer: "Usted está más embrujada que la fregada. Su comadre le pagó a la otra pa que hiciera esto y que lo otro. Y si no quiere creer, tómese esta pastilla." Pues sí. "Y cuando le ponga de ella, que pase eso, mire cómo va a echar usted un bonche de cabello asina." Y sí. Ya esa píldora estaba rehecha para ese fin. Pus un sustazo que llevaba la enferma, que sanaba en veces del susto. Y munchas cosas parecidas a ésas vi yo. "Va a echar uñas; va quién sabe qué, con una cabeza." Y el enfermo siempre estaba con la esperanza. No importa qué le dijieran los vendedores a un enfermo. Todo era güeno. Ai los agarraban.

No podían los vendedores hablar con los de Gualupe en inglés porque la gente no les iba a entender. Hacían lo posible.

A eso iban. Un diandante, eso tiene que tener. Tiene que ser lépero, astuto. Tener, como dicen ellos, *what it takes!* Tiene que ponerse chango uno. Entre más chango es, mejor vendedor. Tiene que vender lo que traiga de un modo u otro. Mi viejito, por ejemplo, no le creiba a naiden, ni a su Padre Nuestro. "Confianza," decía, "ni a mi agüelo."

Peddlers

Adrián Chávez

These peddlers from the Río Grande Valley here in Albuquerque who used to go to Guadalupe had a habit of deceiving its people. Nothing was sold with the assurance that it would turn out to be good. And let's not even talk about cosmetics for women: creams and all of that stuff. Many women got to purchase any old pomade, let us say, and then they'd buy a bunch of small bottles but only the labels on them were different. The peddlers would put the same thing in all of them. They'd sell you two or three bottles for your skin.

Then there were those who tried to play doctor; they went over to Guadalupe to cure people who had been bewitched and things like that. Everything was prepared beforehand here in Albuquerque. That's why I say that things such as dealing in witchcraft required training. There's pills, many different kinds. A lady would be told: "You're more possessed than all get out! Your *comadre* paid another *comadre* to inflict this evil and so forth on you. And if you don't want to believe it, take this pill." Sure enough! "And when you take it and pass whatever is wrong with you, mark my word, it's going to be a ball of hair like so." And sure enough! The purpose of the pill was a foregone conclusion. Why the patient sometimes got well from the mere shock of seeing what he supposedly had passed! I witnessed many things like what I just described. "You're going to discharge fingernails; you're going to discharge who knows what bearing a head." As a consequence, the poor patient was always hopeful of positive results. It mattered not what the peddlers told the patient. Everything was good, in their estimation. That's how the patients were duped.

The peddlers were not able to communicate in English with the residents of Guadalupe because the people simply weren't going to understand them. The peddlers did the best they could.

They had a reason for going to Guadalupe. One must have a bit of devil in him. You have to be a cheat and shrewd. You must have, as they say, what it takes. You have to be on the ball. The wiser you are, the better salesman you make. One way or another you sell whatever you're peddling. My old man, for example, didn't believe anyone, including his own prayers. "When it comes to trust," he used to say, "I don't even trust my grandfather."

Nos atemorizaron

Alberto Salas

Aáen el Río Puerco se originó primero ese *Grazing Division* ladiao que tuvimos y tenemos aquí mismo en Albuquerque ora. Ésos vinieron y empezaron a limitar a la gente con los animales. Nos hicieron matar en un tiempo. El gobierno, traiban orden del gobierno, esos *rangers* que le dicían, como el Cas Goodner y ésos. Vinieron, y el Strong, que era el jefe del Departamento del *Grazing Division*, vinieron y nos atemorizaron. Hicieron *threaten* de que las vacas se iban a morir y que teníanos que matar y tiralas. ¡Un fregal de vacas!

¡Qué insulto era ése! *That was the worse* que ha pasao en la historia de los rancheros.

En papá una vez mató como veinte y cinco vacas que no necitaba de habelas matao. Al cabo si se morían por falta de pasto pus nomás se perdían. Ellos, los *rangers*, no perdían nada. Pero ellos traiban la ley; y ellos traiban el rifle. Y el mismo gringo: "¡Paum! ¡Paum! Aquella otra. ¡Paum, paum!" Ai en el corral mataron . . . Oh, mamá estaba llorando. Se quiso volver loca, por sus vacas. Hasta podía haber matao a en papá, por haber convenido él. Ella no quería. Podía habelo matao ella, de sentimiento y de coraje. Porque esos ladiaos *rangers* vinieron y hicieron a en papá que matara un fregal de vacas ai.

Y loo aquí estamos con el tiro de caballos jalándolas pa los arroyos a tiralas, contoy cuero. No valían ni el cuero. Los *rangers* mismos las mataban. Ellos mismos. Este Goodner usaba la arma. Ai delante: "¿A cuál quieres matar? ¿Aquélla? ¡Toma!"

La razón que daban era que no iba a ver pasteo. ¿Qué les importaba a ellos? No estando enfermas. No había enfermedá en esos tiempos. Estoy posible que sería como del '37 al '38, por ai.

El Goodner era *ranger* de los terrenos del gobierno, y él mismo mató las vacas. Atemorizaba a los pobres vaqueros. Les decía:

—Tienes tantas vacas *over-grazing*.

Ése era el punto y *toavía* es. Si no se ha acabao. Él le decía a uno:

—Oye tú, hombrei, hombrei. Tú tienes muche vaca. Noh pasteo. Está tú violándole. I'm *from the* Grazing Division, hombrei.

Pus los pobres gentes de ai atemorizaos. "Si no quitas esto o lo otro te lo vamos cancelar *todo*."

Ai está, ¿ves? *Threatening the people.* Era muy sucio el negocio en ese tiempo y toavía está. Toavía está el BLM. ¡Uh! Son unos . . .

We Were Humiliated

Alberto Salas

It was over in the Río Puerco where we first had that crooked Grazing Division and we still have something like it right here in Albuquerque. They came and started cutting back the number of animals people could have. At one time they made us kill some of them. From the government, they had orders from the government, the rangers so-called, such as Cas Goodner and the rest. They came, along with Strong who was head of the Grazing Division, they came and humiliated us. They threatened us that the cattle were going to die so we had to kill them and dispose of them. It was a bunch of cows!

What an insult that was! That was the worst thing that's happened in the history of the rancher.

My dad one time slaughtered about twenty-five cows and he didn't have to kill them. Anyway if they died due to lack of pasture they simply died. The rangers weren't going to lose anything. But they had the law on their side; and they had the rifle too. And the same gringo went about shooting: "Bang! Bang! That one over there. Bang, bang!" There in the corral they killed . . . Poor mom was crying. She almost went crazy over her cows. She could even have killed my dad, for having given in to the rangers. She didn't want to go along. She could have killed him, from grief as well as anger, because those crooked rangers came and made my dad kill a slew of cows.

And then here we were with the team of horses dragging them to the arroyos to dump them, hide and all. They weren't worth the price of their hide. The rangers themselves killed them. They did so themselves. This man Goodner used his firearm. There you are: "Which one do you want to kill? That one? Bang!"

The reason they gave for killing them is that there was going to be a shortage of pasture. What did they care? As long as the cows weren't sick. There were no illnesses at the time. I'm sure this was from about 1937 to 1938, thereabouts.

Goodner was a ranger in charge of grazing lands, and he himself slaughtered the cows. He used to torment the poor cowboys. He'd tell them:

"You have so many cows over-grazing."

That was the point of contention and *still* is today. Why it hasn't changed. He'd say to you:

"Listen here *hombrei, hombrei*. You have too many cow. No pasture. You violating law. I'm from the Grazing Division, *hombrei*."

That's how the poor people were humiliated. "If you don't remove this cow or that one we're going to cancel your grazing permit."

There you are. Threatening the people. It was a dirty business then and still is. There's still the BLM to contend with. Oh! They're a bunch of . . .

El dijunto Sotero

Nasario P. García

Una vez aquí en El Empedrao que le nombran, llegaron estos dos
hombres, porque este hombre, el dijunto Sotero, tenía una
laguna. Y ai llegaban los pasajeros, los que iban de aquí de la
plaza, de Alburquerque, pa que me entiendas, pal Río Puerco, y
los que iban en carro de bestias y a caballo, ai paraban y les
cobraba tanto el dijunto Sotero por dales agua. Asina vivía él. Y
tenía cuarto pa los pasajeros allá en la casa onde vivía él. En ese
tiempo había un hombre ai, que estaba viviendo con él que iba
pasando. Güeno, llegaron éstos. Eran dos gringos, que
sospechaban que el dijunto Sotero tenía dinero. Vinieron ya no
sé a qué horas de la noche y ai en la cama onde estaba le dieron
un balazo. No sé en qué parte. Quizás pensaron que tenía dinero
pero no jallaron nada. De ai lo sacaron, y estaba un pino juera
cerca de la casa, ai lo colgaron. Pero no lo horcaron; lo colgaron
nomás. Quizás a ver si les dijiera si tenía dinero o no. El hombre
éste que estaba con el dijunto Sotero, quizás sintió todo. De ai, el
hombre éste, cuando vido lo que estaban haciendo, lo que
habían hecho, salió corriendo a caballo y jue a dar parte. Y allá
toda esa mesa pal otro lao de El Empedrao, ai vivía su hijo del dijunto Sotero. Cuando ya vino su hijo, junto con el hombre este
que te digo, ya aquellos hombres que balearon al dijunto Sotero
ya se habían ido. Su hijo lo jalló colgao patas pa arriba pero toavía
estaba vivo.

Ése era el dijunto Sotero de ai de El Empedrao.

The Late Sotero

Nasario P. García

Once upon a time here in El Empedrao (Stone Pavement), as it's called, these two men arrived, because this man, the late Sotero, owned a lake. And travelers used to stop there, those who were en route from Albuquerque, just so you understand what I'm saying, to the Río Puerco; and, those on horsewagon or riding on horseback, stopped there and the late Sotero would charge them so much for water. That's how he earned a living. And he also offered lodging in his house where he lived. At that time there was a man staying with him over night, who was passing through. Well then, these two men arrived. They were two *gringos*, who thought the late Sotero had money. They got there. I don't know what time of the night it was but there where he was sleeping they put a bullet in him. I don't know exactly where. Perhaps they thought he had money but found nothing. From there they dragged him out of the house. Close to the house there was a pine tree. That's where they hung him, but they didn't kill him. They only hung him upside-down. I guess they did it to see if he would tell them whether he had money or not. The man who was staying over night with the late Sotero, I guess he heard everything. Henceforth, this man, when he saw what they were doing, that is, what they had done, he took off on horseback to spread the word. On that mesa on the other side of El Empedrao, there lived the late Sotero's son. When his son arrived, along with this man I'm telling you about, the men who had wounded the late Sotero had already taken off. His son found him hanging upside-down, but he was still alive.

That was the late Sotero from El Empedrao.

Se pintó

Adrián Chávez

El señor este era muy decidido, como le platiqué antes de las vacas y todo eso, y era medio atroz. Le gustaba muncho el *good time*, yo creo. En una ocasión se robó una señora y la llevó a un rancho; aá estuvo.

Después volvieron a Gualupe por él y cuando lo jueron arrestar, salió a juir. Lo siguieron un día, el chota que había aá y unos cuantos hombres, pero que se les jue. Se anduvo muncho ajuera. Después volvió y empezó a trabajar ai con este Miller onde trabajaba el agüelo de usted. Pues cuando ya supieron que estaba ai, mandaron a dijir al alguacil que lo agarrara. ¡Pues sí! Aquel hombre jue y buscó unos cinco hombres más, yo creo, aá en Gualupe, que hasta mi viejito andaba ai en bonche con un *shotgun*. Se vinieron al rancho ai a esperalo, al rancho de José Miller. Y se escondieron estos hombres pa esperalo, ¿ves? ves. Sabían que él tenía que regresar. Pues en la tarde, esa tarde cuando regresaba este Eduardo Baca, y su agüelo de usted, don Teodoro García, que venía con él, y otro hombre . . . Cuando llegaron a la puerta del cerco, allí al rancho, no sé si su agüelo de usted o el otro hombre, es que le dijo:

—Parece que hubo gente hoy aquí en el rancho.

—¿Por qué?—es que le dijo.

—Sí—le dice—. Hay demostraciones.

Esa gente se fijaba en todo, ¿eh? Estaba retiradita la casa, pero se dieron cuenta. De manera que cuando iban llegando, ya que estaban cerquita, como en el patio, salieron estos hombres y les pusieron los rifles a ellos. Y el caballo de este Eduardo Baca nomás se paró así derecho, enfrente donde le estaban apuntando el rifle a él, y es que parecía que estaba embalsamao aquel caballo. Estaba bien parao asina pa arriba. Y querían matalo a este Eduardo Baca, pero al fin unos con otros convinieron de que no lo mataran, porque había uno de los hombres—yo creo que ése era el que se sentía más injuriao—pues que quería matalo. Le dijo el compadre:

—No—es que le dijo—tenemos que agarralo, agarralo y llevalo vivo.

Pues sí. Ya lo agarraron esa tarde y lo amarraron, que el dijunto José Márez jue el que lo veló, porque en otra ocasión se les había juido, teniéndolo ya. El suegro de mi viejito que me crió lo cuidaba la vez anterior. No, y se les escapó. Pero en esta otra vez pusieron a este José Márez y es que "a mí no se me va, sólo que me vaya junto con él." Se lo amarró, yo creo. Que otro día lo trajo pa Bernalillo este Márez. Pues tamién a José Márez se le escapó una vez antes de ésta, cuando lo llevaba en el bogue, quizás lo llevaba suelto. ¡No! Por ai donde le dicen La Cueva, usted sabe ónde es eso, ai estaba la cequia y todo eso. Y este José Márez venía con un par de mulas fanfarronas, y le arrebató este Eduardo la pistola. Tiró dos tiros y arranca. Pues este Eduardo tenía que tener . . . porque a José Márez lo echó en la cequia y él se pintó por otros dos años o no sé qué.

Y jue a La Pinta este Eduardo. Aá estuvo muncho tiempo. Después salió y ya estaba poco más manso. Ya nomás robaba pocas vacas ai en Gualupe, como le platiqué la vez anterior; iba pa Lincoln.

Después era un viejito muy güeno. Ai estaba; no mataba una mosca. Después que ya pasó toda la cosa del rancho, es que le preguntaron:

—Eduardo, ¿cómo sabías tú que había gente en la casa?

—Porque cuando abrimos la puerta del cerco, diuna vez me fijé que estaba la lanza de uno de los carros o bogues caida.

Ellos siempre la tenían amarrada, ¿ves? ¡Pues ellos se fijaban en todo! Estaban yo creo con el delito en la mente.

He Ran Away

Adrián Chávez

This man, Eduardo Baca, was very assertive, as I told you when speaking about how he stole cows and all of that. Fact is, he was a bit reckless. I guess he liked to have a good time. One time he stole a woman, took her with him to a ranch, and kept her there.

Afterwards the authorities came to Guadalupe for him and when they went to arrest him, he escaped. One day he was pursued by a sheriff and a few other men, but, believe it or not, he ran away from them too. He spent a lot of time away from Guadalupe. Later he returned and started to work there, in Guadalupe, with this man named Miller where your grandfather used to work. Once the authorities found out that he was there, they sent word to the sheriff to catch him. Sure enough! The sheriff formed a possee of five men, besides himself, I believe, from there in Guadalupe. Even my father was among them, with a shotgun. The sheriff's possee came to Joe Miller's ranch to wait for Eduardo Baca. You see, these men were lying in wait. They knew he had to return. Well, that afternoon as he was returning, along with your grandfather, don Teodoro García, who was with him, plus another man. When they approached the gate at the ranch, I don't know if it was your grandfather or the other man who said to Eduardo Baca:

"It appears that we had visitors here at the ranch today."

"Why do you say that?" he said to him.

"You can tell," he said. "There is evidence."

Those people took notice of everything, ah? The house was still a bit far away from the gate, but they realized something was amiss, so that as they were approaching the house, since they were pretty close, like at the patio, the possee came out and pointed their rifles at them. About that time all that Eduardo Baca's horse did was to stand straight up on its hind legs, right in front of where they were pointing their rifles at him. It looked as though that horse was embalmed. He was standing straight up. And the possee wanted to kill this Eduardo Baca, but finally they agreed among one another not to kill him. Apparently in the group there was one man—I believe he was the one who felt the most humiliation—who wanted to shoot him. His compadre said to him:

"No," he said, "we have to catch him, catch him and take him in alive."

Sure enough! That very same afternoon they caught him and tied him up. In fact, it was the late José Márez who watched over him, because on another occasion Eduardo Baca had run away from them; this was after they already captured him. My father's father-in-law who raised me, had guarded him the previous time. No matter, he escaped just the same. But on this other occasion they selected this José Márez who boasted that "he won't run away from me, unless he takes me with him." I believe he tied him to himself. On the following day this man Márez brought him to Bernalillo, the county seat. You see, Eduardo Baca had run away from José Márez once before, when he was taking him in on a horse carriage. I guess he had him loose. Then, wouldn't you know it! Around a place called La Cueva (The Cave), you know where that is, there was a ditch and that sort of thing. And this José Márez had a couple of swaggering mules when all of a sudden Eduardo snatched away from his pistol. He fired two shots and off he went. I would say that this Eduardo had to have had . . . because he threw José Márez into the ditch and ran away for another two years, or what have you.

Eduardo ended up in the penitentiary. He spent a lot of time there. Later he was released and by then he was already much tamer. He would only rob a few cows there in Guadalupe, as I told you on a previous occasion. He'd go to Lincoln County, to sell them.

Afterwards he was a very nice little old man. There he was; he couldn't kill a fly. Much later, long after the possee's episode at the ranch, he was asked:

"Eduardo, how did you know there was someone home?"

"Because when we opened the fence gate, I right away noticed that a pole of one of the wagons was on the ground."

You see, they always had it tied. Why they noticed everything! I guess Eduardo invariably thought he was going to be murdered.

Robándose la campana de la iglesia

Benjamín "Benny" Lucero

Bien. Yo jui el que puso el rifle pa quitásela, pa que la golvieran patrás y la pusieran onde debía estar. Yo jui el que los agarré.

Cuando estaban quitando la campana de la iglesia, andábanos a caballo, andaban dos vecinos míos conmigo: el Resti Sandoval y Matías García. Andábanos al sur del Río Puerco, pal otro lao del Cabezón, cuando vimos unos individuos andar arriba del techo de la iglesia. Eran cinco individuos los que andaban. Eran de la universidá. Cuando llegué a onde estaban ellos . . . yo jui el primero que llegué a onde estaban. Este Resti se arrendó por unas bandejas porque le estaba dando queque a unas vacas. Pero este Matías García me siguió. Cuando llegué a onde estaban ellos les pregunté que si quién les había dao el poder, y me dijieron que no, que esto y aquello. Me contaron una historia ellos, que no era de nadien esa campana y que por eso la iban a mudar. Les dije que se arrendaran y pusieran esa campana pa arriba, porque ya la habían bajao hasta la sacristía. No hicieron caso.

Me golví, pronto bajé, pronto pa la casa y agarré mi rifle. Yo tenía un 25-20. Cuando venía llegando a la casa, me arrimé a la pader. A una pader. Ai estaba uno de ellos cuidando a mi esposa. Ya ella estaba mirándolos por la ventana de la casa quitar la campana pero no se les arrimaba porque les tenía miedo. Como digo, cuando llegué yo ya estaba un individuo atrás de una pader con una pistola cuidándola a ella. ¡Pártole en el caballo! Y en ese tiempo llegó el Resti, y le dice, le dice el Resti:

—Diles a tus compañeros que se arrienden y pongan esa campana. Ve ayúdales a tus compañeros a poner esa campana patrás—le dijo.

El de la pistola no jallaba qué hacer con ella. Podía habernos matao a nosotros. Antonces les dice a los compañeros:

—Tenemos que poner patrás esta campana.

Eran dos los que estaban con la campana; otro estaba dentro

de la iglesia; y el otro estaba con el carro listo en la última casa, pal poniente, pa salir a juir con ella. Estaba con el carro listo, pa cuando abajaran la campana ellos, antonces cargan la campana. Pero no pusieron la campana patrás. La acarrearon y se jueron par onde estaba el carro. El carro salió pal poniente. Antonces agarramos nosotros una troca y dimos la güelta por el levante y los topamos y agarramos la licencia.

Y luego nos vinimos y los siguimos hasta San Ysidro. Y tráibanos la licencia nosotros. De ai llamamos a los oficiales de Bernalillo, del Condao de Sandoval, en el telefón. Llamamos que esos individuos andaban haciendo robo de la campana. Cuando los arrestaron, los encerraron. Les quitaron dos dagas y dos pistolas, o tres pistolas y dos dagas. Y luego ellos llamaron pacá pa Alburquerque y pusieron fianza y salieron.

Cuando juimos a la corte, juimos a un arreglo, que nos dieran mil quinientos pesos pa reformar la iglesia, en arreglo. No salió de ese modo. Al fin ellos comenzaron a poner tacha de que no tenían dinero y pacá y que pallá y que primero los iban a encerrar y que no íbanos a sacar nada más. Que nos daban cien pesos dijieron. Jue yo creo que trabajo de los mesmos, de los mesmos oficiales que estaban ai. ¡Política! Y dijieron que nos daban los cien pesos, y al mesmo tiempo cuando nos jueron a dar los cien pesos, metió una mujer que era de allá del pais, la dijunta Beatriz Heller, metió su voz ella ai que no nos dieran los cien pesos a nosotros. Nosotros queríanos los cien pesos siquiera pa poder atrancar la iglesia y hacer unas reformas de ella. Dijo la dijunta Beatriz Heller que le dieran los cien pesos al arzobispo en donación.

Después agarré la campana de la case corte, porque no tenía nadien onde salvar la campana. Y yo la metí; yo jui el que la metí a un *safe*. Y la tengo en un *safe*, la campana. Y han venido con amenazas, me las han echao algunos, que entregue esa campana. Que la campana la quieren pa donala pa la iglesia de Jémez Springs. ¡Y no la ha entregao; y no la entrego!

También nosotros tenemos en el Cabezón iglesia. Cuando yo compré el terreno, la iglesia estaba en el terreno mío. Y asina es.

Stealing The Church Bell

Benjamín "Benny" Lucero

Okay. I'm the one who pointed the rifle at them to take the bell away from them, so they'd return and put it where it belonged. I'm the one who caught them.

When they were removing the bell from the church, we were on horseback, two neighbors and I: Resti Sandoval and Matías García. We were toward the south of the Río Puerco, on the other side of Cabezón, when we spotted some individuals walking around atop the church. There were five of them. They were from the university. When I got to where they were . . . I was the first one there. Resti had gone back after some pans because he was feeding the cows cake. But Matías García followed me. When I got to where these characters were I asked them who had given them authority to be there, and they mumbled one thing or another. They made up a story, to the effect that the bell belonged to no one and that's why they were going to remove it. I ordered them to turn back and to put the bell back up in its place, because they had already lowered it to the sacristy. They paid no attention.

I went back, quickly, toward the house, and I grabbed my rifle. I owned a 25–20 (Winchester 94). When I was approaching the house, I got close, I got close to one of the walls. There was one of those characters keeping an eye on my wife. She had already been watching them, through the window, take down the bell but she didn't dare get close to them because she was afraid of them. As I say, when I arrived one of those guys was already behind a wall with a pistol watching over her. I went after him with my horse! About that time, Resti got there, and Resti says, he says to him:

"Tell your friends to turn back and for them to put back the bell. Go help them put that bell back," he said to him.

The one with the pistol didn't know what to do with it. He could have killed us. Then he says to his friends:

"We have to put the bell back."

Two were with the bell; another one was inside the church; and, the other one had the car ready, on the west side of the village, ready to escape with the bell. He had the car going, so that when they brought down the bell, then they'd load it up. And they didn't put the bell back. They carried it instead and headed for the car. The car took off in a westwardly direction. Then we climbed on a truck and went around eastwardly and ran into them and took down the license's number.

Then we took off and followed them until we got to San Ysidro. We had the license's number with us. From there we called the officials (Sheriff's Office) in Bernalillo, from Sandoval County. We got in touch with them about those characters who were stealing the bell. After they were arrested, the sheriff locked them up. The officers found two daggers and two pistols on them, or was it three pistols and two daggers? Then these guys called Albuquerque, secured a bond and were set free on bail.

When we went to court, we had a deal in mind, that is, for them to give us one thousand five hundred dollars to fix up the church. It didn't turn out that way. In the final analysis they started to give as an excuse that they didn't have money, this or that, and that they'd be locked up first before we got anything else out of them. They said they'd give us one hundred dollars. I believe it was a ploy concocted by the same officials who were there at the trial. Politics! They said they'd give us the one hundred dollars and about the time they were going to do that, a woman who was from Cabezón, the late Beatriz Heller, she put in her two cents, for them not to give us the money. We wanted the one hundred dollars at least to secure the church and fix it up a little. Instead the late Beatriz Heller suggested that the one hundred dollars go to the archbishop as a donation.

Afterwards I picked up the bell from the courthouse, because no one had a place for safeguarding it. And I was the one who,

who put it in a safe. And I have it, the bell, in a safe. And some people have come here with threats; they've threatened me, to hand over the bell. That they want the bell to donate it to the church in Jémez Springs. But I haven't handed it over; and I won't.

We have a church in Cabezón also. When I bought the land, the church was on it. And that's the way it is.

Votaban hasta los muertos

Damiano Romero

¡La política era otra cosa! Nos prometían muncho los políticos. Aquellos políticos de Bernalillo o dionde juera, republicanos o demócratas. Prometían muncho, que iban hacer un puente en el Río Puerco, que iban a componer los caminos, que iban hacer beneficio. Pus hablaban muy bonito y todo. Cuando ya votaba uno por ellos, que ya estaban sentaos en las oficinas, ya no le ponían atención al pais.

Pues como es lugar chiquito, les hablaban ai mismo en la junta, que tal día iba a ser la eleción. Antonces votaba uno por boleto, por papel. Ponían jueces de un partido y de otro y era tanto, güeno era tanto—muncha gente no sabía—que votaban hasta los muertos. Y nunca se sabía nada pero un muerto ya hacía diez años que se había muerto, y toavía estaba ai en el libro. Alguien votaba por él—los oficiales votaban. Nunca se sabía qué pasaba. Había más votos de un partido que de otro y era que estaban votando todos los muertos. Nunca los llegaron agarrar pero había prebas de que votaban hasta los muertos. Era pura política, puro negocio.

Otra cosa. Los políticos más altos, de aquí del Condao de Sandoval, pagaban a personas ai en Gualupe. Tengo razón, porque eran algunos de mis tíos. Se me hace que no era muncho dinero, pero les daban cien pesos pa que le dieran a la gente pa que votara. Ciertas gentes se quedaban con los cien pesos; no le daban ni un *pene* a la demás gente, a los demás pobres. Daban cien pesos pa que repartieran, dígase, en veinte personas o lo que juera, unos cinco pesos cada uno.

Esa persona se quedaba con too y no dijía nada, que no le

había dao ayuda a naide ni nada. De modo que al que le daban dinero pa ayuda, ai nomás se quedaba con él y no le daba a los demás pobres. Nomás votaban porque querían votar.

Venía cada quien por su voluntá. Tenía que venir él mismo en su costo, en su caballo. Allá no los llevaban a votar.

Even The Dead Voted

Damiano Romero

Politics was something else! Politicians used to promise us many things, whether they were from Bernalillo or wherever, Republicans or Democrats. They promised lots of things, like that they were going to construct a bridge on the Río Puerco, that they were going to fix the roads, that they were going to help people out. It was nothing but pretty talk. Once you voted for them, and they were in office, they no longer paid any attention to that country.

Since it was a small place, politicians spoke to the people right there in the political rallies concerning election day. Then you voted by paper ballot. Judges from both parties were set up, but it was so bad, it was so bad—many people were unaware—that even those who were dead got to vote. And it was never revealed, but at times a dead person had already been dead for ten years, and his name was still on the books. Someone would vote for him—the election officers. You never knew what went on. There were more votes cast for one party than the other and it was because dead people were voting. Those responsible for casting such votes were never caught, but there was proof that even the deceased voted. It was pure politics, nothing but connivance.

Something else. The more influential politicians, from Sandoval County, they'd give money to certain individuals in Guadalupe to get the vote out. I know, because some of these individuals were my own uncles. I don't believe it was a lot of money, but politicians would give them one hundred dollars to give to the people so they'd vote. Some of these characters kept the one hundred dollars; they wouldn't give one cent to the rest of the people, to the poor. The politicians gave one hundred dollars, let us say, to have them divided among twenty people or whatever number, about five dollars per person.

The so-called contact person often kept all the money and said nothing about not having given anything to anyone. Fact is, the person who received the money for distribution, simply kept it and wouldn't share it with the rest of the poor folks. These people voted simply because they wanted to vote.

Every individual went of his own volition. He went at his own expense, on horseback. People weren't coaxed into voting.

Buenos vaqueros

Benjamín "Benny" Lucero

A lo que yo me acuerdo, me acuerdo muncho de don Teodoro García. No, no amansando caballos, pero me acuerdo porque era hombre muncho mayor que yo. Ya era hombre viejito él, hombre muy anciano pa lo que yo me acuerdo.

Pero me acuerdo de tu papá, Nasario García. En casos, que llegué a ver caballos reparar con él. ¡De los güenos! Te digo que él era una de las güenas personas que yo vide. Un caballo, pon tú un caballo en apariencia, de volencia y carrera, y que se te haga reparar, ésa es una sorpresa de una persona. Él (Nasario) una vez en un caballo, partióle a un becerro y lázalo, y el caballo se clavó a reparar. ¡De ai sácate tú que tan güeno no era! ¡Qué lo vide yo! Nomás no lo movió; nomás no lo movió. Y todavía desató el cabresto de la silla, reparando el caballo, pa que no lo enredara. Eso lo vieron mis ojos ai en La Laguna del Número Dos, que le dicen. ¡Güen vaquero!

Otro güen vaquero que vide, que rechazó, jue el dijunto Macario Romero. También a volencia de carrera, vólcase el caballo con él, y salir corriendo adelante del caballo él. ¡Qué tal güeno no era!

Eso es lo que vide yo cuando hacían los rodeos ai en esos lugares pa marcar. Tú estarías muy chiquito. Al que llegué a ver jue al Galo, tu primo hermano. A ése lo traiban en caballitos mansitos.

A otro también que te digo que lo vide una vez en volencia y carrera, pa que alcanzara a brincar un tusero, jue a en papá. Veníanos en pues de unos caballos que venían juyendo, y pícale al caballo al pasar pa que alcanzara a brincar un tusero, y cuando pasó el tusero se clavó a reparar con él. Él mesmo le dio güelo a las riendas pa que alcanzara abrincar el tusero. Ya era hombre viejo. También le doy crédito porque no lo tiró el caballo. Te digo que le jaló las riendas, que le quemó los guantes, y quedó con la punta de las riendas nomás. Hasta que paró el caballo de reparar.

Güeno, también a Cirilio García. Era güeno, güeno pa andar a caballo. Muy güeno, Cirilio, de los vaqueros más güenos de ese pais.

El Tone Gardía, llegó a ensillar un caballo bronco par un rumbo y yo par otro. Pero yo no me quiero dar la fama porque es muy malo darse la fama con la boca propia, pero te voy a dar la fama del Tone. Él jue muy güeno. Y su hermano Lizardo también. Llegué a ver yo caballos broncos con ellos. Y otro hermano, el dijunto Rubo era güeno. Le voy a dar crédito a esa familia, a cuatro de los hermanos que yo los vide con mis ojos. Esos Gardías: eran Rubén, Lizardo, y un compadre mío, Jesióstomo, y este Tone Gardía. Los otros dos menores, ésos no anduve con ellos, pero con aquéllos sí anduve.

Y loo teníanos otro vaquero que cayó ai en ese pais con vacas. Le dieron derecho de vacas en La Mercé. David Padilla se llamaba. Ése era un hombre muy al tanto. Ése si lo llegué a ver yo con mis ojos. Un caballo reparar de arriba de un cerro, venirse pa bajo reparando con él, ¡y no volcarse el caballo!

Yo sí vide munchas cosas donde anduve. Anduve entre los navajoses. ¡Cómo los navajoses no hay! Y todavía te digo la verdá. Ésos son unos gatos. Son más que gatos. Un gato clava las uñas en una cosa y no se suelta. Nomás no se suelta. Asina son los navajoses. ¡De los mejores! Yo anduve entre ellos; ha andao entre los navajoses más de lo que ha andao entre los mejicanos. En cosas de ésas, de caballos. También en travesuras anduve con ellos, que hasta la fecha tengo amigos en los navajoses, lo mesmo que tengo amigos mejicanos.

Yo llego hoy a una casa de un navajó, amigo mío, es mi casa. Me tratan, igualmente que mi gente. Y anduve en fiestas de los navajoses, toda clas de fiesta, cuando amansaban caballos. Ora no. Ora no. Ora si vas tú se te rodean de puros tomoviles. En aquellos años se rodeaba de carrería de caballos que hasta trompezaba uno con las lanzas de los carros de caballos. Y los caballos, algunos se espantaban, reparaban en medio de todo ese lancerío y carros de caballos. ¡Y la navajocería gritándoles! Nomás por pasar el rato. Cosas bonitas; cosas que vide que si ha habido una cámara, ora valieran muncho dinero esos retratos.

Estaba la gente en los modos antiguos. Lo mesmo que había modos antiguos entre los mejicanos había entre los navajoses. Muncho anduve yo con los navajoses, como dije antes. Nos juntábanos, encerrábanos caballadas y par ellos no había color ni tamaño. Ni casi le dijían a uno, "¡Deténmelo!" Algunos jineteaban con el sarpingo nomás. Ponían el cabresto enredor de la panza. Otros nomás con la clin enredada en la mano. Sin freno. Y te digo, que hasta hacían corrales en los arroyos.

Llegué a ver casos yo . . . una vez un caballo se soltó reparando. Llegó a la orilla de un arroyo y el caballo se cayó pa bajo y se mató y quebró la silla y el navajó se salió pal otro lao.

A ésos les llamo yo gente que sabía usar el mente, cómo salirse de un caballo. ¡Qué tal livianos no! Yo los llegué a ver. Terribles. Y todavía ora les digo yo de los navajoses a mis hijos: "Mira éste, éste es uno de los que llegamos a andar juntos y lo llegué a ver yo con mis ojos hacer esto y esto."

Y les digo, les pongo en acuerdo, les digo a mis mesmos amigos míos, los navajoses. "¿Te acuerdas de esto?" "Sí. Sí me acuerdo." Y se ríen. "¡Qué tal tontos! ¡Cómo no nos mataron los caballos!"

Ora están tan enfermos esos navajoses. Quién sabe si más de lo que estoy yo. Ora están tan religiosos que tú los miras y dices: "Esto que me está platicando es una mentira." Están tan religiosos, tan resentaos, a antes del modo que vivían ellos en el hogán, en el ramada; o echar su lumbre ajuera y unas saleas de colchón y no importa que las estrellas temblaran de frío. Dormían tapaos y quizás el mesmo vapor adentro de la qüilta, la frezada, se calentaban porque dormían ondequiera.

Good Cowboys

Benjamín "Benny" Lucero

From what comes to mind, I remember a lot about Don Teodoro García. Not with regards to breaking horses, but because he was a man quite older than me. He was a pretty old man, quite old from what I can recollect.

But I remember your dad, Nasario García, from situations in which I got to see him on bucking horses. He was one of the good ones! I tell you he's one of the best bronco riders I ever saw. A horse, take a horse, as a for instance, that's high kicking, and running, and you make him buck, that's a sign of a good cowboy. Nasario was once on a horse, and he took off after a calf, roped it, and the horse dug in and started to buck. You decide from that how good he was! Why I saw him! The horse simply didn't shake him lose; it simply didn't! And he was still able to untie the rope from the saddle so he wouldn't get all tangled up, all of this while the horse kept on bucking. I saw that with my own eyes at La Laguna del Número Dos (Lagoon Number Two), as it was called. Good cowboy!

Another good cowboy I saw, who excelled, was the late Macario Romero. Picture a horse kicking high and running, plus over-turning with him on it, and still end up running ahead of the horse itself. Imagine how good he was!

That's what I saw when they held round-ups in those places (the Río Puerco) during branding time. You must have been very small. The one I remember seeing was Galo, your cousin. They had him on very tame horses.

Someone else I also saw one time on a high kicking horse as it jumped a prairie dog mound was my dad. We were after these horses that were running away from us, and he spurred his horse as it came upon a prairie dog mound so the horse could jump over it, and in doing so, it started bucking with him on. He himself let the reins lose so the horse could jump the prairie dog mound. He was already an old man. I give him credit because the horse didn't throw him off. I'm telling you, he pulled on the reins, burning his gloves in the process, and in the end all that he had left was the tips of the reins. Until the horse stopped bucking.

Very well then, there was also Cirilio García. He was good; he was good on horseback. Cirilio was very good, one of the best cowboys from the Río Puerco country.

Tone Gardía, he once saddled a bucking horse going one way and I the other. But I don't want to take the credit because it's bad to brag about yourself, but I'll boast about Tone. He was very good. And his brother Lizardo also. I got to see them on wild horses. And another brother of theirs, the late Rubo, he was good. I'm going to give that family credit; four of the brothers I saw with my own eyes. The Gardías: they were Rubén, Lizardo, and a compadre of mine, Jesióstomo, and this Tone. There were two other younger brothers, but I didn't run around with them, with the other ones I did.

And then we had another cowboy who showed up with cattle in that country of ours. The government gave him permission for grazing cattle in La Merced. David Padilla was his name. That man was on top of things. Him I got to see with my own eyes. A horse bucking from the top of a peak, and doing so all the way down with him on, and still the horse didn't turn over!

I saw lots of things where I ran around. I ran around with the Navajos. There's none like the Navajos! And I can still attest to that today. They're like cats. They're more than cats. A cat digs its paws in something and doesn't let go. He simply won't go. That's the way the Navajos are. They're some of the best! I ran around with them; I've run around with the Navajos more than with my Mexican compatriots. That is, when it came to matters related to horses. I also cut-up with them, so much so that even to date I have friends among the Navajos, as I do among my own people.

Today if I stop at a Navajo's house who's a friend of mine, his house is my house. They treat me the same as my own people do. And I attended Navajo fiestas, all kinds, such as when they broke in horses. Not anymore. Not anymore. Nowadays if you go visit them they surround you with cars. Years ago you were surrounded with a string of horse wagons, so many in fact that you'd stumble into the wagons' poles. As for the horses, some would get startled and start bucking in the midst of all those wagons and aggregate of lances. And here was the whole Navajo clan shouting at them (the horses). They did so just to pass the time of day. Beautiful things; I saw things that if there had been a camera, those pictures would be worth a lot today.

People were set in their old ways. Just as there were old customs among my people; so were there among the Navajos. I ran around a lot with the Navajos, as I said before. We'd get together and lock up herds of horses, and for the Navajos the color or size made no difference. They barely said to you: "Hold it for me!" Some would break in the horses using only the *sarpingo*. Others put the rope around the horse's belly. Still others all they did was to grab ahold of the mane in one hand. No bridle. And I'm telling you, they'd convert arroyos into corrals.

I got to see cases . . . once this horse cut loose bucking. It came to the edge of an arroyo and the horse went tumbling down, killed itself and broke the saddle, and the Navajo riding it escaped the other direction.

Those are people I like to think as having known how to use their head, such as how to escape from a horse that's in trouble. Just imagine how quick these Navajos were! I got to see them. They were daring. Even now I tell my sons and daughters about the Navajos: "Look at this one, he's one of the ones I ran around with and I saw him do this and that, with my own eyes."

And I tell them, I apprise my children, I tell my own friends, the Navajos. "Do you recall this?" "Yes. Yes I do." And they laugh. "Boy we were crazy! It's a miracle the horses didn't kill us!"

Now those Navajos are so ill. Perhaps even more so than I am. Now they're so religious that if you see them you have to wonder: "What this man is telling me is a lie." They're so religious, so weakened, compared to before when they lived in their hogans, in their sheds, or outside by a fire using an animal's hide for a mattress no matter if the stars were trembling from the cold. They slept covered up and perhaps the steam (breath) from underneath the quilt, from the blanket, warmed them up because they used to sleep any old place.

Eduardo Baca

Adrián Chávez

Pa montar a caballo, allá en Gualupe nunca hubo naiden que
pudiera hacer lo que hacía Eduardo Baca. En una mula que juera,
que nunca la había tocao naiden, que estaba bronca, mesteña, la
lazaba él y se subía en ella en pelo. Parecía que estaba sentao en
una silleta. Nunca hubo un animal que lo tirara, y reclamaban,
por ejemplo, que juera de aquí él, de Alburquerque, en un
caballo pallá, pal rancho, si se le fatigaba el caballo o algo, ai
mismo es que encerraba un atajo de yeguas, sin corral, sin nada.
Tiraba luego su silla y su subadero, y ai es que se andaban aquellos animales que parecía que andaba la cosa mala atrás de ellos. Y
él agarraba el que quería y lo ensillaba.

Hay munchas historias, munchas pláticas, de ese hombre:
Eduardo Baca. Ya está él difunto. Allí cerquita de El Coruco, allí
cerquitita vivió munchos años. Estaba muy quemao, muy paseao.
Tenía muncha fama. Tuvo muncho nombre. Jue atroz cuando su
tiempo. Pero ya después que estaba anciano, ya en nuestra familia
lo conocimos nosotros de paz, muy buenazo. Muy mansito estaba. Pero jue muy hombre en su tiempo; hasta jue a la prisión,
dos, tres veces. Tenía que haber sido muy entrón pa hacer lo que
hacía.

En aquellos años, más allá había unos Mora, ai en Gualupe;
tenían munchas vacas. Pos es que les robaba a ellos ciento cin-
cuenta, doscientas vacas y se iba hasta el Condao de Lincoln. De
por allá era él. Allá las cambiaba; de allá traiba otras tantas y se
las vendía a los Mora. Todo eso tenía él con los ricos. Pero no,
con los pobres era muy güena gente él. Mayormente cuando se
hizo viejo; hasta un ataque le daba. Ai caiba, se levantaba y
seguía. Me vía a mi cuando tenía yo como unos diez y siete años.

—¡Y caray!—me dijía—. Así como tú vine yo aquí a
Gualupe. Tavía no tenía *bozo*.

Muy curioso. Llegué a platicar muncho con él. No se mal gastaba el tiempo uno con él. Siempre estaba uno ocupao.

Eduardo Baca

Adrián Chávez

As far as riding on horseback is concerned, in Guadalupe there was never anyone who could do the things Eduardo Baca did. Even if it were a mule that no one had ever ridden, broken in or wild, he'd rope it and get on it bare back. It looked like he was sitting on a chair. There never was an animal that could buck him off, and people claimed, for example, that in case he were to be headed for Guadalupe from here in Albuquerque on horseback, toward the ranch, if his horse tired on him or something, right there he'd lock up a herd of mares, without a corral or anything. He'd throw his saddle and saddle blanket to one side, and those animals were beside themselves as though some evil thing were after them. He'd grab whichever one he wanted and saddle it.

There are many stories, a lot of talk, concerning that man: Eduardo Baca. He's already dead. Right there close to a place called El Coruco (The Bedbug), right close is where he lived for many years. He was quite burned out and very well traveled. He was well known, and had made a name for himself. He was very daring in his heyday. But afterwards when he was old, by then those of us in our family knew him as a peaceful and very good man. Very meek. But he was quite a man in his prime; he even ended up in prison, two or three times. He must have had a lot of guts to do what he did.

Back then, a long time ago, there were these Moras, in Guadalupe. They had many cattle. Well, I understand that he'd steal one hundred-fifty, two hundred cows from them and he'd head for Lincoln County. That's where he was from. That's where he'd trade them and return with an equal number and sell them to the Moras. He only did that sort of thing to the rich folks. As far as poor people were concerned, not so. He was very good to them, especially when he got to be old. He even suffered from some kind of a fit. He would fall, get up, and continue. He used to look at me when I was about seventeen years old.

"Good grief!," he'd say. "I was your age when I came to Guadalupe. I didn't even have a mustache."

He was very amusing. I got to chat a lot with him. Time went by very fast with him around. He kept you entertained.

2

Tragedies

Whether in fiction or in real life, tragedy has always been a part of man's seemingly hostile environment. Tragedy epitomizes man's troubles, according to Ogden Nash, but death, unlike other tragedies, is the most prevalent.

The inhabitants of the Río Puerco Valley were by no means spared from either tragedy or death. In many ways one could argue that their region, while it was alive, was a microcosm of tragic events typical in the daily lives of farmers and ranchers. Stories of tragedies in the Río Puerco Valley abound; some of these are recorded in this chapter.

When a tragedy occurred, as it often did in those times, it was accepted as "the will of God" (*así lo quiso Dios*), and the family as well as the community drew closer together to help one another. This can particularly be seen in "Tragedy after Tragedy," where Emilia Padilla-García, who was my paternal grandmother, had lived in several different households between the time she was a baby and when she was married at thirteen years of age.

The Río Puerco, which was once vital to the welfare of the people along its banks, also often played havoc with their lives. Drownings such as those depicted in "The Two of Them Drowned" were not uncommon, and, when they occurred, the entire community united to mourn the loss.

The height of tragedy and its traumatic consequences can best be appreciated in "Influenza" a dramatic account by Luciano Sánchez that takes us back in time to the influenza epidemic of 1918. Conversely, "A Scar" by Salomón Lovato, while it may lack the tragic aspects present in other stories, the potential for tragedy, possibly even death, is indeed present.

Ruperto Gonzales, a local hero, though a *persona non grata* in the eyes of the law, died at the hands of the authorities. An even more tragic death occurred west of Cabezón (my father and I visited the site in 1985) at the beginning of this century. Juan Valdez was brutally axed to death. Versions of his murder vary, but it has become legendary in the minds of many Río Puerco Valley residents.

Tragic events like the two alluded to here were not easily forgotten. I, for example, have known of Juan Valdez's death since I was six years old. Tragedies of this type and those like Ruperto Gonzales's many times resulted in the composition of ballads (*corridos*) in their honor. These ballads, imbued with tragic overtones, contributed in large measure toward keeping stories of misfortune alive in a community for years to come.

Tragedia tras tragedia

Emilia Padilla-García

Nosotros juimos residentes en Pecos. Allá jui nacida yo, pienso, en Pecos. Mi papá mío lo mató el tren, recién de que empezó a entrar el tren. Allá en Pecos. Porque mi papá y otros estaban trabajando y venían a traeles provisión a sus familias. A la casa. Se llegó día sábado que vino mi papá, Antonio se llamaba, Antonio Padilla, que vinieron a traele comida a mamá él y su cuñao. Antonces comenzaba el tren hacer tráfico, quizás. No sé qué año sería. Yo estaba muy chiquita, estaba muy chiquita yo toavía.

Y venían en una de esas ruedas, ¿cómo le dicen? ¿Tranvías? Ai venían a traeles comida. Y creo que en la güelta asina de una, de una mesa o no sé qué sería, ellos venían y el tren iba, y ai los pescó. Los mató a los dos.

Allá en Pecos quedamos nosotros. Quedé yo güerfanita, chiquita, junto con mi hermanito Antonio y una hermana mía que se llamaba Virginia, y mamá. Mamá era de los Tafoya, de mamá grande. Allá quedamos.

De Pecos nos trujieron a Corrales, pero allá se quedó todo. Todo se quedó. Pero yo no puedo saber qué años en aquel tiempo. Estaba muy chiquita yo. Muy chiquita estaba. Y, como digo, ai estuve en Corrales. Ai me estuve con mi mamá grande y loo tócame la mala suerte que muérese mi mamá grande. Me quedé con una tía y un tío. Solitos los tres; quedamos güérfanos.

En el año de 1897 murió mi tío Florencio, el que me crió. Antonces como mi tía quedó viuda, mi tía Eremita, nos juimos con su mamá, mi mamá Vidal. Nos juimos con ella a Salazar; allá en su casa nos estuvimos. Allá jue onde me casé yo, en Salazar, con Teodoro García. Allá lo jui a conocer yo a él. Muy jovencita me casé hijo, de trece años entraos a catorce. Yo estaba murre muchachita.

Tragedy After Tragedy

Emilia Padilla-García

We were once residents of Pecos. I believe that's where I was born, in Pecos. There in Pecos is where the train killed my dad, right after the trains started running. My dad and others were working on the railroad and they were on their way home to take food to their families. It was a Saturday when my dad, Antonio was his name, Antonio Padilla, was on his way home, along with his brother-in-law, to take food to my mother. That was, perhaps, the beginning of the railroad. I don't know what year it was. I was very small; I was still very little.

Anyway, he was riding one of those carts, what do you call them? Trams? That's what they were riding on their way to deliver the groceries to their families. And I believe it was on a curve, a curve that rounded a mesa or I don't know what it was, so that they were coming and the train was going, and that's where the train caught them. It killed both of them.

In Pecos, that's where we were left without a father. I was left a little orphan with only my little brother Antonio and a sister of mine, whose name was Virginia, to live with my mother. Mom was from the Tafoya family, on my maternal grandmother's side. Pecos is where we were left fatherless.

From there we were brought to Corrales, but everything we had stayed back in Pecos. Everything was left behind. But I can't tell you what year that was. I was quite small. I was very small. And, as I say, I spent some time in Corrales. I stayed there with my grandmother and then I'll be darned if my grandma didn't die. I was taken in by an aunt and an uncle. We were all left alone; all three of us were left very much alone.

In 1897 my uncle Florencio, the one who raised me, died. Then, since my aunt became a widow, Eremita was her name, we were taken in by her mother. Mom Vidal, we called her. We went with her to Salazar; that's where we lived. That's where I got married, in Salazar, to Teodoro García. That's where I got to meet him. Son, I was very young when I got married; I was thirteen going on fourteen. I was barely a young girl.

La influenza

Luciano Sánchez

Yo como en el año 1918, casi en ese tiempo abrí los ojos. Jue cuando comencé a refaicionar todo. Me acuerdo de esa enfermedá yo en el rancho. Éranos seis que estábanos enfermos y nos juimos casi todos. Ai caí yo y murieron más de cinco en casa. Creo que a esos cinco los enterraron en un joyo: la dijunta María, el dijunto Diopoldo, la dijunta Lucía, el dijunto Salomón y mi agüelito. Unos eran tíos; otros eran primos. Lucía era mi tía; Salomón era mi tío. El dijunto Jesús Sánchez era mi agüelito. Y Diopoldo y María eran primos hermanos.

Andábanos visitando otras gentes del Río Puerco cuando se enfermó mi tío primero y de ai se enfermó mi tía y loo de ai siguieron los dos hijos de él. Y antonces él y yo juimos y trujimos los caballos pa irnos a la casa. Yo le ayudé a echar todos los enfermos y nos juimos. Yo iba arreando. Cuando llegamos aá a un descanso que le dijían más tarde El Descanso de la Dijunta Idalia, ai me pegó a mí. Y ya no supe nada hasta que llegamos a la casa.

Y ai en la casa me acuerdo que estaba mi otra agüelita mía, por la parte de mamá, y le dije a la otra agüelita que se iban a llevar a mi hermanita Juanita. Ya yo no supe más. Murieron todos los de la casa y no supe hasta que yo no sé cuándo me levanté. Yo no supe si me curaban o no me curaban. La única cosa que me acuerdo es que una mañana que venía saliendo el sol, iban cantando cuatro hombres con una mujer a enterrala. Nomás cuatro hombres. No más gente, no más nada. Era una vecina de nosotros ai que le decíanos la dijunta Idalia. En ese tiempo me levanté como de un sueño, de la cama y estaba una mesa asina onde estaba la ventana. Puse una silleta y loo me subí arriba de la mesa y ai me senté a ver pa juera. No había ni un barullito en casa; no había naiden. Nomás cuatro hombres iban con esa mujer a enterrala, cuando entró mi agüelita y me dice:

—Hijito. ¿Qué estás haciendo ai?

—No—le dije—. Oí cantar un alabao y me subí pacá arriba.
Y ya dijo:

—¡Apéate de ai; te vas a cae!

Y ai me estuvo diciendo que habían muerto todos los de en
casa, junto con mi hermanita Juanita y mi agüelita. No quedó ya
más de una agüelita y en papá.

Yo me sentí muy triste por una cosa, porque mi prima hermana María quizás me quería muncho. Porque yo era huérfano
de madre. Ella me quería muncho; ella me lavaba; ella me vestía.
Y en ese tiempo había munchos piojos. Ella me espulgaba; ella
me pelaba. Y loo la dijunta Lucía lo mesmo. Y el dijunto Salomón
siempre andaba conmigo. Él siempre me traiba pa ondequiera. Me
sentí solo. Me sentí triste. En casa no quedaron más de dos. Tres,
comigo.

Influenza

Luciano Sánchez

It was around 1918 when I barely opened my eyes. That's when I began to reflect on everything. I remember that particular illness at the ranch. There were six of us who were ill and just about all of us died. I came down sick, and more than five died at my house. I believe all five were buried in one plot: the late María, the late Diopoldo, the late Lucía, the late Salomón and my dear grandfather. Some were aunts and uncles; others were cousins. Lucía was my aunt; Salomón was my uncle. The late Jesús Sánchez was my grandfather. And Diopoldo and María were my cousins.

We were visiting some people on the Río Puerco when my uncle got sick first, and from then on my aunt, followed by my uncle's two boys. So then he and I went and fetched the horses and hitched them to the wagon to go home. I helped him load up everyone who was ill and we took off. I was driving. When we got to a place where a person had died, which came to be known as El Descanso de la Dijunta Idalia (A Cross-Bearing Place Where the Late Idalia Died), there I was stricken with the same illness. I didn't know what hit me until we got home.

I remember that my other grandmother, on my mother's side, was at home, and so was my paternal grandmother, whom I told that God would not spare my little sister Juanita. That was the end of me; I didn't remember anything else after that. Practically everyone at home died and I didn't come to find out until I woke up. I don't know when that was. I had no idea whether I was given medical attention or not. The only thing I recall is that one morning as the sun was coming out, four men, singing, were on their way to bury a woman. Only four men. No more people, no more anything. She was a neighbor of ours whom we called Idalia. It was about that time that I woke up, like from a dream. There was a bed close to where the window was. I put a chair and climbed up on top of the table and started to look outside. Not a single whisper could be heard at home; nobody was home. Only four men were carrying that woman to bury her, when suddenly my grandmother came in and said:

"Hijito. What are you doing there?"

"Why nothing," I said to her. "I heard someone singing a hymn of praise and I climbed up here."

Then she said:

"Get down from there; you're going to fall!"

Then she commenced to tell me how everyone at home had died, along with my little sister Juanita and my grandmother. The only people left were one of my grandmothers and my father.

I felt very sad. For one thing, my cousin María evidently liked me a lot, because I didn't have a mother. She liked me very much: she'd wash me; she'd dress me. Lice were very common at that time. Consequently she would clean me; she would cut all of my hair off. And the same thing was true of my aunt Lucía. Also, I was always with my uncle Salomón. He always took me everywhere. Thus, I felt alone. I felt sad. Only two people at home survived. Three, counting me.

Se hogó un muchacho

Perfilia Córdova

El Ojito de Gualupe, no sé si se acordarán las muchachas o tú, tiene un cañón. Es un cañoncito. De eso sí me acuerdo yo bien. Y don Juan Córdova hizo un atarque ai en El Ojito de Gualupe pa represar la agua pa que pudiera uno sacala. El Ojito de agua güena está par un lao. No se me olvida. De ai salía la agua fría, *tan* fría como si hubiera tenido hielo. Y par el otro lao corría la agua del cañoncito ese pero ésa salía salada y como mojo. Estaba como mojosa.

Don Juan tamién hizo una cequiecita al lao del atarque y la agua corría pa bajo; y le hizo a la gente de Gualupe un tanque pa la agua güena. Nosotros mesmos carreábanos agua de ai, pus no teníanos que tener barriles pa carrear la agua como la gente que vivía lejos de El Ojito.

En ese lugar de Gualupe, onde nosotros vivíanos, arriba de la mesa, un poco retirao de la placita, tamién estaban unos tanques de piedra, como unos aguajes, pa que me entiendas. Y ai íbanos nosotros cuando caiba agua; íbanos a trae agua pa beber o pa lo que juera. Corría la agua de un cerro, o no sé diónde correría esa agua, y caiba al tanque ese grande. Ai jue onde se hogó un muchacho, en ese tanque. Un muchacho de por ai de Juan Tafoya.

Estos muchachos estaban con unas borregas. Estaban en ahijadero. Y había dos muchachos: este Climaco y otro. Y es que viniendo es que les dijo el caporal:

—Váyanse con los atajos.

Güeno. Salieron ellos con los atajos. Y el caporal este se jue a huachalos y vido que se arrendó este Climaco y el otro no. El otro siguió con su atajo. Y es que le gritaba aquél a Climaco, de arriba de la mesa:

—Vente hombre. Allá viene el caporal.

—No—es que le dijo.

Pues se desvistió pronto Climaco y se dejó ir pa dentro del tanque. Se jue a la profundidá. Porque ese tanque no sé, yo no sé
ónde tendría el plan, pero no lo podían sacar a Climaco.

Estuvo mi compadre Samuel, estuvo don Juan Córdova,
munchos, haciéndole lucha y no pudieron sacalo. Hasta de-
saguaron el tanque aá arriba; lo taparon, pa que me entiendas.
No lo pudieron sacar. Al fin tuvieron que ir con mi compadre
Mariano, su apá de Adelita Gonzales. Ése lo sacó. Me acuerdo
como si ora juera.

No tragó agua el muchacho. No más que . . . lo que hubo es
que yo creo que a éste le dio dolor de corazón porque estaba
muy fría la agua. Y luego pues pegó en una piedra y se le atoró
un pie. Asina investigaron ellos: mi compadre Samuel Córdova,
don Juan Córdova y los demás. No sé. Pero lo sacaron; lo sacaron
con la ayuda de mi compadre Mariano.

A Young Man Drowned

Perfilia Córdova

El Ojito (The Small Spring) in Guadalupe, I don't know if either you or your sisters remember, but El Ojito in Guadalupe is in a canyon. It's a tiny canyon. That much I do recall very well. And don Juan Córdova constructed a small dam right in El Ojito in order to hold back the water so people could draw it out. El Ojito containing the good water is to one side. That I don't forget. The water from there used to come out cold, *so* cold as if it had had ice. And on the other side, the water from the tiny canyon that I'm telling you about, it came out salty and like rust. It tasted rusty.

Don Juan also built a small ditch to one side of the dam and the water ran downstream; and he erected for the people of Guadalupe a tank for the good water. We ourselves used to haul the water from there, inasmuch as we didn't have to have barrels to haul the water the way people who lived far from El Ojito did.

In Guadalupe itself, where we used to live, on top of the mesa, a little ways from the village, one could also find several earthen rock tanks, like whirlpools, so that you'll understand me. And that's where we'd go whenever it rained; we'd go fetch water for drinking or for any other purpose. I don't know where that water came down from, whether it came down from a peak or what, but it would drop right into that large earthen rock tank. That's where this boy drowned, in that tank. The boy hailed from Juan Tafoya or some place like that.

You see, these boys were tending to their sheep. It was during the breeding season. There were two boys: one named Climaco and another one. And on the way their foreman I guess told them:

"Go on along with the two flocks of sheep."

Very well. The boys accompanied the two flocks of sheep, and their boss decided to keep an eye on them and saw that this Climaco turned back but not the other fellow. The other guy proceeded with his sheep. The story goes that he was hollering at Climaco from atop the mesa:

"Come on man. There comes the foreman."

"Oh, don't worry about it," so he responded.

Well, Climaco quickly undressed and let himself go smack into the water tank. He went to the deep end, because as far as that tank is concerned, I don't know where the bottom could have been, but the fact is that they couldn't pull him out.

My compadre Samuel was there, don Juan Córdova was there, and many others, all of them trying very hard, but they were still unable to pull him out. They even emptied the water tank farther on up; they stopped the water from coming in, so you'll understand better what I'm saying. They still did not succeed in taking him out. Finally they had to go after my compadre Mariano, Adelita Gonzales's father. He pulled him out. I remember that as if it were now.

The young man didn't swallow water. The only thing is that . . . what happened, I believe, is that this fellow suffered a heart attack because the water was very cold. And then, to make matters worse, he bumped his head against a rock and one of his feet got stuck. That's what they were able to ascertain: my compadre Samuel Córdova, don Juan Córdova and the rest of them. Who knows how they did it, but they pulled him out. They did so with the help of my compadre Mariano.

Llegaron con el cuerpo

Salomón Lovato

Te voy a platicar otro chasco que me pasó en el cemeterio de San Luis. ¿Quieres que te lo platique?

Sabes que en el tiempo de la *depression* estaba tan pobre la gente y abrió el gobierno los CC *Camps*. Y cayó una lluvia muy grande aquí en Socorro; pienso que era pal tiempo que se jue San Marcial. Y este primo mío se lo llevó la agua y se hogó, ¿ves? Como se hogó Frank Jaramillo también aá; también estaba en el CC *Camp*. Y este, este primo, no lo jallaron hasta como dos meses después. Ya estaba casi deshecho.

Y jueron estos oficiales pan casa, no pan casa, pan casa de la gente del muerto y me llamaron a mí porque la gente no sabía hablar el inglés. Y me dijieron los oficiales, dijieron que no metieran el cuerpo a la casa, que tenían que enterralo de una vez. Y no estábanos más de yo y otros dos hombres allí. Había gente pero estaba trabajando, ese día, y llegaron los oficiales con el cuerpo y nos vieron a nosotros a que juéranos a sacar el sepulcro. No estaban más de tres hombres.

Y ya estaba pa meterse el sol, y pus no había eletricidá. Nomás llevamos un farol. Y comenzamos a sacar el sepulcro—estos tres hombres. Y loo ya el sepulcro estaba ya muy bajito, estaba bajito, y me metieron a mí, y comencé a sacar más el sepulcro y cuando menos acordé me jui. ¡Pa bajo! Y me agarré con las uñas, pus ya estaba noche. Yo pensé que me había agarrao alguien de abajo de la tierra, pus hay munchos sepulcros. ¡Y qué rebato llevé! No te miento que agarré la tierra con las uñas y me prendí, y me sacaron de abajo. Me enfermé, oye, del rebato. No toqué plan; me jui pa bajo. ¡Hijo!

They Arrived With The Body

Salomón Lovato

I'm going to tell you about another incident that happened to me at the San Luis cemetery. Do you want me to tell you about it? You know that during the depression people were so poor that the government started the CC Camps. About that time a torrential rain fell in Socorro; I believe it was about the time that San Marcial was washed away. And, you see, this cousin of mine was also swept away by the current. Frank Jaramillo was also drowned; he was working at the CC Camps. But they didn't find this cousin of mine until some two months later. His body was practically dissolved.

These government officials went to my house, not to my house, to the relatives of the deceased, and I was called over because the people didn't know English. So the officials informed me not to let the people take the body in the house, that they had to bury it right away. I and a couple of other men were the only ones around there. There were other people in the village but they were working that day, so the officials got there with the body and spoke to us about digging the grave. There were only three of us around.

The sun was about to go down and there was no electricity. The only thing we took along was a kerosene lantern. We started to dig the grave, the three of us. Pretty soon the grave was really deep, quite deep, and they got me in to dig. I started to dig more of the grave when all of a sudden I disappeared. Way down! I grabbed ahold with my fingernails; it was already dark. I thought someone had grabbed ahold of me from underneath. You see, there's lots of graves. It scared the living wits out of me! I'm not lying to you; I grabbed ahold of the side of the grave with my fingernails and held on until they pulled me up. Listen, I got sick from the incident. I didn't hit bottom; I went down. Wow!

Se hogaron los dos

Eduardo Valdez

Éste era un hombre, marido de la dijunta Seferina Armijo. Eh, siempre ellos tenían cabras, y tenían un corral en un lao del Río Puerco, onde encerraban las cabras. Y luego del otro lao del Río Puerco estaba la casa, onde residían ellos. Y en la mañana un muchichito como de unos diez a quince años, yo creo, cuidaba estas cabras a caballo. En la mañana jue el muchichito en su caballito, echó las cabras y las cuidó todo el día. Y en la tarde cuando ya tenía que encerralas vino y en esto bajó un crecientón en el Río Puerco. El papá cuando vido esto, nomás que no me acuerdo cómo se llamaba el papá, pero cuando vido esto—era muy güen nadador—nadó y cruzó el río pal lao que estaba el muchichito. Agarró al muchichito y lo subió en el caballo y agarró las riendas del caballo y se golvió a echar otra vez pal lao de la casa, pa cruzar el río, pero la agua sacó al muchichito de la silla. Y poco abajito de dionde lo sacó al muchichito hacía un remanse la agua cuando estaba corriendo, en el río. Y el papá vido al muchichito que se estaba volteando allí en la agua, y se echó a socorrelo, y se hogaron los dos.

Antonces la agua se los llevó a los dos. La corriente se los llevó, y el hombre no sé si el mesmo día o qué tantos días después, lo jallaron poco abajo dionde se había hogao, y el muchichito no lo jallaron. Al fin ya se habían cansao de buscalo, y ya no lo buscaban. Antonces, como quince días aá bajo de aquel lao de la placita esa que toavía le nombramos Casa Salazar, había un redamadero muy grande—en varias partes del río, había—pero ai había un redamadero muy grande en el río, que cuando bajaba agua en el río, redamaba la agua y dejaba muncha leña. Y la gente teníanos costumbre de, cuando bajaba agua asina en el río, y que se paraba, juntábanos la leña que traiba el agua, porque traiba muy güena leña, de todas clases.

Un hombre, Agustín Armijo, de ai de Salazar, jue un día *muncho* después de que pasó esto que te digo de este muchichito y este hombre que se hogaron. Muncho tiempo después jue él a juntar leña en ese redamadero. Había munchos álamos, álamos muy altos. Él anduvo juntando leña y echándola en el carro y al fin se cansó—estaba calor, creo, decía el dijunto Agustín—y se acostó abajo de un álamo a sombrear y a descansar. Se acostó boca arriba y a ver pa arriba del álamo, cuando vido al muchichito en una horqueta del álamo, como treinta o cuarenta pies arriba del álamo.

Antonces cuando lo vido luego él se acordó de este muchichito, que se había hogao en días pasaos. Antonces es que se levantó y al tiempo de su levantada, se horrizó muncho, el hombre este Agustín. Antonces es que le dijo él al muchito: "¡Ah carajo!," es que le dijo. "¡Mira! Déjame ir y no te voy a dejar! Voy a avisar pa venir por ti."

Y asina es que pasó en esa vez.

The Two Of Them Drowned

Eduardo Valdez

This man was the husband of the late Seferina Armijo. Ah, they always had goats, and they had a corral on one side of the Río Puerco, where they locked up the goats. Then on the other side of the Río Puerco was the house where they resided. One morning a little boy of about ten to fifteen years of age, I believe, was taking care of these goats on horseback. In the morning the little boy went on his horse, let the goats loose and herded them all day long. In the evening when he had to lock them up he came to cross the river and about that time a huge flood came down the Río Puerco. When the father saw this, except that I don't recall the father's name, but when he saw this—he was a good swimmer—he swam and crossed to the other side of the river where the little boy was. He grabbed the little boy and put him on the horse and grabbed the reins and jumped in the water again facing the house, to cross the river, but the water forced the little boy from the saddle. A little ways down the river from where the little boy was sucked up, the water turned into a whirlpool whenever the river ran. The father saw the little boy going round and round in the water, and jumped in to save him and both drowned.

Then the water washed both of them away. The current carried both of them, and the man, I don't know if it was the same day or how many days afterwards, was found a short ways down river from where he had drowned. As for the little boy, they didn't find him. Finally they got tired of looking for him, and gave up. Then, down the river on the other side of the little village we still call Casa Salazar, there was a large spillover—this was true in many sections of the river—but at this particular spot there was a very large spillover, so that when the river ran, it overflowed and left a lot of wood. And people had a habit, whenever the river ran and then stopped running, of gathering the wood that the water carried, because it brought along very good wood, all kinds.

A man, Agustín Armijo, from Salazar, went one day long after all of this happened that I'm telling you about the little boy and this man who drowned. This man, Agustín Armijo, much later went to gather wood from this spillover. There were lots of trees, very tall trees. He went about gathering wood and loading it in the wagon until he got tired—it was hot, I believe, so said the late Agustín—so he lay down under a tree to take in the shade and rest. He lay down face-up looking at the tree, when he spotted the little boy in one of the tree forks, about thirty to forty feet up the tree.

Then when he saw him he thought of the little boy who had drowned in days past. Then I understand he got up and, upon doing so, he, this man named Agustín, became very frightened. Then he is to have said to the little boy: "Oh, what in tarnation!," so he said to him. "Listen, I'll be right back; I won't leave you here! I'm going to spread the news so we can come after you."

And that's the way it happened, a long time ago.

El barranco los trampó

Eduardo Valdez

Éstos eran hijos del dijunto Pedro Ramírez. Así se llamaba el
papá, hijo del dijunto Martín. Eran de esos Ramírez que había en
Gualupe. Y este hombre, Pedro, vivía en un rancho de Gualupe
aá arriba. Bueno, vamos a decir que como unas seis, siete millas
paá arriba. Un día que había misa ai en Gualupe, scría domingo o
no sé qué, se vino toda la familia a la misa, en un carro o am-
bulanza nueva que tenía el dijunto Pedro. Vinieron a la misa aquí
a Gualupe. Antonces estuvieron en la misa y cuando se acabó se
jueron. Pa llegar a su casa de este hombre Pedro, como una milla
de distancia, pa llegar a la casa, hay un arroyo que le
nombrábanos, y le nombran toavía, El Ojo de Las Yeguas.

Había caido una lluvia aá en la sierra y esta gente cuando gol-
vieron pus no, no sabían ellos que había caido esa lluvia pallá.
Llegaron al arroyo ese, estaba hondo. Bajaba el camino derecho y
subía derecho. Cuando bajaron, que bajaron los caballos abajo del
arroyo, llegó el crecientón de agua y de una vez los volteó a los
caballos pa bajo. Tuvieron la chanza todos de brincar patrás
toavía juera del agua. Y se jue el carro contoy caballos. Se los
llevó la agua y poco cerca de ai está el golpeo onde cae el arroyo
ese pal río, pal Río Puerco. Ai cayó el carro contoy caballos. Y
hacía un remanso onde caiba la agua. Ai se quedó el carro, en ese
joyo, y los caballos se desengancharon, de güena suerte, y salieron, pero ai se quedó el carro.

Antonces esta gente cuando ya se bajó la agua del arroyo, pasaron todos a pie. Ya no estaba muy lejos la casa. Te digo que
como una milla, o fácil menos. De una milla pa llegar a la casa.
Cuando llegaron a la casa, les contaron a los muchachos que se
habían quedao allá en casa, que era lo que les había pasao, y ellos
se jueron y vieron que el carro estaba allí en el joyo ése. Toavía
estaba caindo agua, poquita.

Pues luego jueron dos de los hijos de Pedro Ramírez, el dijunto

Eulalio, y Conrao Ramírez, era su hermano. Y luego jue uno tamién que estaba casao con una hermana de ellos, se llamaba Alfredo, Alfredo Martínez. Era de estos Martínez, de Márquez.

Bueno, dijieron ellos que venían a ver si sacaban el carro. Iban a desbaratalo y sacalo en pedazos. Estaba nuevo. Se metieron el dijunto Eulalio y el dijunto Alfredo. Se metieron a desbaratar el carro y a sacalo en pedazos, y nomás en cuanto bajaron y estaban desbaratándolo cuando se les vino el barranco y los trampó.

De güena suerte que el hermano menor, Conrao, se había quedao arriba del barranco. Cuando se les cayó el barranco a los otros, éste partió pa la casa avisar, que los había trampao el barranco. Luego vino a ver toda la familia y hicieron de una vez por juntar gente pa sacalos, pa sacalos muertos, pus ya no había más chanza. Es que se tardaron cuarenta y ocho horas pa sacalos, pa desbaratar los barrancos y descubrir hasta que los sacaron. Porque tú sabes que esos barrancos del Río Puerco son *brutos* pa desbaratalos.

Bueno, pus los desbarataron con muncho trabajo; muncha gente es que vino a auxilialos, a ayudales hasta que los sacaron.

¡Y asina es que pasó! ¡Y asina es que jue!

The Edge of the River Bank Trampled Them

Eduardo Valdez

These boys were sons of the late Pedro Ramírez. That was the father's name, son of the late Martín. They belonged to those Ramírezes who used to live in Guadalupe. And this man, Pedro, lived on a ranch up north from the village of Guadalupe. Well, let's say that about some six or seven miles up north.

One day that Mass was being celebrated in Guadalupe, it must have been Sunday or I don't know what day, the whole family headed for Mass, in a horse wagon or a new carriage that the late Pedro had. They came to Mass here in Guadalupe. Then they stayed for Mass and when it was over they left. To get to Pedro's, this man's house, about a mile away from the house, there's an arroyo we used to call—and still do—El Ojo de las Yeguas (The Mares' Spring).

It had rained up in the sierra and these people when they returned, why they didn't, didn't know that that rain had fallen up that way. They got to that arroyo, it was deep. The road was straight down and straight up. When they went down, when the horses went down the arroyo, the flashflood struck them and immediately turned the horses over. Still they all had a chance to jump backwards away from the water. And the wagon was swept along with the horses. The current carried them away, and a little ways from there, there's a waterfall where that arroyo empties into the river, the Río Puerco. That's where the wagon fell right over with the horses. And there was a whirlpool where the water fell. That's where the wagon got stuck, in that hole, and the horses luckily became unhitched, and came out of the water, but the wagon remained there.

Then these people, when the water in the arroyo had receded, they all crossed on foot. The house was not far away. I bet it was only about a mile, maybe even less. When they got home, they told the boys who had stayed back what had happened to them, and they took off and saw that the wagon was in that hole. It was still raining a little.

Well, then two of Pedro Ramírez's sons, the late Eulalio and Conrado Ramírez, his brother, went. And then there was an individual who was married to one of their sisters, his name was Alfredo, Alfredo Martínez. He went also. He was one of those Martínezes from Márquez.

Very well then, they said that they had come to see if they could pull out the wagon. They were going to dismantle it and bring it out piece-by-piece. It was new. The late Eulalio and the late Alfredo went in the water hole. They went in to take the wagon apart and to bring it out piece-by-piece and, no sooner had they gone down and were dismantling it when the edge of the river bank overcame them and fell on them.

Luckily the younger brother, Conrado, had stayed above, on top of the river bank. When the edge of the river bank fell on the others, this Conrado took off for home to tell them that the river bank had fallen on them. Then the whole family came to see and immediately they tried to gather people to unearth them, to take them out dead, why there was no other alternative. I understand it took them forty-eight hours to dig them out, to break up the river bank until they dug them out. Why you know that those river banks on the Río Puerco are brutally difficult to break up.

Okay then, it was a lot of work, but they broke them up. Many people presumably came to lend a helping hand, to help them until they were able to dig them out.

And that's what happened! And that's the way it was!

Chapter 2: Tragedies

Una cicatriz

Salomón Lovato

Todos teníanos nuestro quehacer: unos tenían que meter agua; otros tenían que partir leña; y otros tenían que dale de comer a las vacas, a los caballos. ¿Qué no ves cómo tengo esa cicatriz? Esa cicatriz la tengo de un caballo que le vendieron al Catron, el dueño de la Mercé, del Ojo del Espíritu Santo.

Me despacharon a dales agua a los caballos al río, ya noche. Y eran, teníanos, como doce caballos. Yo tenía quizás como unos doce, diez años. Pus, no podíanos sentarnos a la mesa hasta que no hacíanos nuestro taller. Yo tenía que ir a dales agua a los caballos. Y jui y les di agua, pero tú sabes como los caballos van, y les dábanos pastura. Ya la pastura estaba lista y too, pero en la puerta del cerco se pararon. Se paró el primero; se pararon todos. Iban hechos chorros. Y iba yo con la cabeza agachada y no me fijé. Y me dio una patada un caballo y me cortó too. Nomás que yo estaba chiquito. ¿No ves que tengo la cicatriz ai?

Siempre me acuerdo que me tocó un pedacito de Catron.

A Scar

Salomón Lovato

We kids all had our chores: some of us had to bring in water; others had to chop wood; and still others had to feed the cows and horses. Do you see this scar? I owe that scar to a horse sold to Catron, the owner of La Merced in the Ojo del Espíritu Santo.

They sent me to water the horses at the river (Río Puerco); it was already dark. And we had, well, we must have had about a dozen horses. I was about ten, twelve years old. Well, we weren't allowed to come to the table to eat until we completed our chores. Mine was to go water the horses. I did so, but you know how after watering them, we would feed them hay. The hay was already ready and all that, but the horses stopped at the gate to the fence. The first one stopped; the rest followed suit. They were all strung out. I was walking with my head down without paying attention, when a horse kicked me and cut me all up. Good thing I was small. Can't you see my scar?

I always remember that I even got a little piece of Catron.

La muerte de Ruperto Gonzales

Bencés Gabaldón

Yo lo conocí tamién a ese hombre, y pues, eh, lo que pasó con él. Este hombre se andaba robando animales y bestias y toitito eso y vendiéndolas. Pero no las vendía par él. Las vendía y le daba el dinero a la gente pobre. Ayudaba a la gente pobre. Y al fin lo agarraron y lo echaron a la penitenciaria. No me acuerdo qué tanto tiempo estuvo él en la penitenciaria pero estuvo aá y luego se juyó y se vino. Se estuvo en el Cerro de Cabezón; estuvo muncho tiempo.

Y loo de ai se jue pa, pa un lugar que le decían La Laguna del León. Se jue contoy mujer; de ai del Cabezón se jue pallá.

Y luego más tarde se vino pacá pal Cabezón, y la mujer venía en el carro, y él venía a caballo. Él venía atrás. La mujer venía adelante. Y lo topó El Pájaro, que le decían. Éste estaba de chota y tenía derecho de que ondequiera que lo topara, agarralo vivo o muerto. Ai lo topó El Pájaro, en La Angostura, en Los Torreones. Ai lo topó. Está la mesa y loo está el arroyo, y el camino al lao. Por ai se topó con él, y este Ruperto no traiba rifle, y aquél, cuando ya lo reconoció, sacó el rifle y lo atravezó. Le dio un balazo; ai lo mató.

Hasta hicieron un corrido:

> Yo soy Ruperto Gonzales
> el padre eterno me crió.
> Al pasar por La Angostura
> El Pájaro me encontró.
> Me hizo levantar los brazos
> y en el corazón me dio.

Me acuerdo de ese verso yo nomás, pero los demás no sé.

Este hombre, Ruperto Gonzales, le debía a un tío mío aquí en San Luis que tenía tienda. Le pidió dinero o no sé qué a mi tío.

Pues esa noche que lo mataron a Ruperto Gonzales, vino, él vino, a case mi tío. Tenía un macho blanco. Ai es que se paró en la puerta—ya lo habían matao—con las manos asina (en el aire). Es que le dijo mi tío: "¿Qué anda haciendo aquí?" "Vengo a pagar el macho, por lo que le debo." Y se despareció.

Eso me acuerdo yo de Ruperto Gonzales.

The Death Of Ruperto Gonzales

Bencés Gabaldón

I, too, knew that man, and well, ah, what happened to him. This man was going around stealing cattle and horses and all of that and selling them. But he didn't sell them for his own profit. He'd sell them and give the money to the poor people. He'd help the poor folks. They finally caught him and put him in the penitentiary. I don't remember how long he spent in the penitentiary, but he was there for a while and then escaped and returned to the Río Puerco. He hung out at Cabezón; he was there for a long time.

And then from there he left for, for a place people referred to as La Laguna del León (The Lion's Lagoon). He took off, wife and all, from Cabezón to this place.

Later on they came back here to Cabezón: his wife on a horse wagon; he on horseback. He was right behind her. The Bird, so-called, ran into him. He was an undersheriff and had the right to capture Ruperto Gonzales, dead or alive, anywhere he ran into him. There in a place called La Angostura (The Strait), in Torreones, that's where The Bird ran into him, face-to-face. There's a mesa and then an arroyo, with the road to one side. Thereabouts is where The Bird ran into Ruperto, who was not carrying a rifle, but once he recognized him, took out his rifle and let him have it. The Bird put a bullet in him; he killed him right then and there.

Someone even composed a ballad about him that went like this:

> I am Ruperto Gonzales
> The Eternal Father created me.
> As I passed thru La Angostura
> El Pájaro ran into me and

Made me put my hands up
And shot me thru the heart.

I recall only that verse, the others I don't.

This man, Ruperto Gonzales, owed some debts to an uncle of mine who had a store in San Luis. He had borrowed some money or I don't know what all from my uncle. Well, it so happened that on the night he was killed, he came to my uncle's home. Ruperto Gonzales had a white he-mule.

Evidently he stood at the door—he had already been killed—with his hands up in the air. So my uncle is said to have commented: "What are you doing here?" "I've come to give you the he-mule in return for what I owe you." And then he disappeared.

That's what I remember about Ruperto Gonzales.

Muere Ruperto Gonzales

Benjamín "Benny" Lucero

Güeno. En papá también platicaba de un individuo, Ruperto Gonzales, que le robó unos caballos. Tocó que en papá agarró dinero trabajando en el estao de Arizona. Cuando vino aquí, al Cabezón, vino con algún dinerito, y compró caballos pa dejárselos a mi agüelo. No era muncho el precio de ellos; un güen caballo lo compraban por doce pesos. Era muncho dinero en esos tiempos, en los tiempos que él estaba joven. Reclamaba que había comprao dos caballos muy güenos, de los caballos mentaos. Se los compró al dijunto Ricardo Heller del Cabezón, que tenía muy güenas bestias.

Güeno, y había un individuo ai, este Ruperto Gonzales, que se robó una señora, y también le robó a en papá los caballos. Luego lo agarraron con la señora ésta, juyendo, lo agarraron por aquí, por aquí en Alburquerque; ai lo agarraron. Lo arrestaron por robos que había hecho más atrás y fregaderas que había cometido él. Güeno. Y este hombre tenía su familia. Y la señora esta cuando lo agarraron se arrendó patrás ella, y los caballos que le había robao él a mi agüelo, los había vendido por aquí en Belén. Lo arrestaron y lo llevaron a la pinta.

Después se juyó Ruperto Gonzales de la penitenciaria. Y este hombre cuando se juyó de la penitenciaria vino a dar a onde estaba su familia. Tenía dos hijos: uno se llamaba Varisto y el otro se llamaba Antonio. Este hombre se anduvo por muncho tiempo juyendo. Ya en papá estaba trabajando con otros en La Sierra, en las borregas. Has oído mentar El Ojo de Chatino, ¿no? Ai estaba.

Dicía en papá que venía Ruperto Gonzales a beber agua y a dale agua al caballo ai en El Ojo del Chatino. En un caballito blanco andaba juyendo él de la penitenciaria. Pus no lo jallaron a él, onde estaba la familia. Éste iba y llegaba, yo creo. Ai venía algunas veces en la noche onde estaba la mujer. La mujer se llamaba Juanita. Y éste se estuvo preparando. A veces dijía en papá que nomás estaba el campo solo y agarraba comida, les agarraba comida del campo. Seguro que se venía a dormir a las piedras. Ai maneaba el caballo en un lugar onde no lo vieran. ¿Ves? Pero dijía en papá que en un lao de la ladera lo vía él cuando llegaba al ojo y bebía agua. Pus éste se estuvo previniendo hasta que se salió porque alguien dio parte de que se había llevao a la mujer y a los dos muchachos. Yo creo que asegún el rumbo que llevaba, él, este hombre, iba pal estado de Arizona.

Hay una laguna que le dicen La Laguna del León. Antonces había la policía montada. Éstos de la policía montada llevaban un hombre, que le llamaban El Pájaro, y estaban sesteando ai en La Laguna del León, pal rumbo de La Gaváchica. Este Ruperto Gonzales ya iba en el camino con un carro de caballos. Su mujer iba arreando el carro de caballos. Arrancó a juir, cuando llegó la policía montada atrás de él. Brincó en el caballo; ni su rifle agarró. Brincó él en el caballo y salió a juir y se jue, que jue cuando le quitaron la familia.

De ai de La Laguna del León, arrendaron los de la policía montada a un rancho. En este rancho había una casa cerca del rancho del dijunto Rudolfo Tachías. Ai campearon. A la mujer la pusieron adentro de la casa, y ellos destendieron las camas en el patio pa podela cuidar. Ella se recogió con los dos muchitos adentro de la casa. Pero este hombre, su marido, arrendó en la noche y vino a onde estaba la mujer. Ella le dio de cenar por la ventana. Luego es que le dijo él: "Ya me voy a entregar. Ya me cansé de andar juyendo," es que le había dicho a la mujer. Platicaba la mujer eso.

De todos modos, este hombre se jue otra vez, pero antes de irse es que le dijo a su mujer: "Si puedes—porque su rifle toavía estaba en el carro de caballos—si puedes," es que le dijo, "en La Angostura," hay un lugar que le dicen La Angostura, viniendo todo el Arroyo del Chico, aquel lao del rancho de don Donaciano, "si puedes me tiras el rifle, del carro de caballos." Por alguna razón no pudo tiralo ella. No le dieron tiempo la policía montada—los que venían con ella. En el rancho de Maque, taa no era de Maque, le dijían La Vega de Marcos, ai sestearon. Ai descargaron la policía montada, me platicaba en papá. Y este Pájaro, que menté antes, era caporal de la compañía, ¿ves? El Pájaro este se arrendó patrás y traiba el rifle cargao. Ai en la mera Angostura topó al dijunto Ruperto. El dijunto Ruperto, pus, lo conoció y le levantó los brazos, donde jue que El Pájaro le dio un balazo en el corazón. El dijunto Ruperto no traiba rifle. Hasta un corrido compusieron de él. Ése lo oí yo en el Cabezón. Dicía—algo de lo que me acuerdo—dicía:

> El Pájaro en La Angostura me encontró,
> me hizo alzar los brazos y en el corazón me dio.

Cerca de ai mesmo donde estaba caminando su mujer y sus hijos, es que había dicho Antonio, uno de los hijos: "Ya mataron a mi papá," porque oyeron el tiro. Como te digo, no estaba muy lejos.

Y sí. El Pájaro se golvió y lo reportó que él lo había matao. Es que se soltó llorando de una vez la mujer.

Ya murió la tía de mi mujer. Ella me platicaba a mí de un hombre, este Tomás Valencia, que estuvo en el velorio de Ruperto Gonzales. Él vido el balazo, el balazo en el mero corazón.

Ruperto Gonzales Is Killed

Benjamín "Benny" Lucero

Now then, my dad also used to talk about this individual, Ruperto Gonzales, who stole some horses from him. It so happened that dad earned some money working in Arizona. When he came here, to Cabezón, he had a little money, so he bought some horses to give to my grandfather. The price wasn't very high; a good horse could be purchased for twelve dollars. That was a lot of money back in those days, back when he was young. He claimed to have bought two good horses, the best known horses around. He bought them from the late Ricardo Heller from Cabezón, who used to have very good horses.

Anyway, there was this individual, Ruperto Gonzales was his name, who stole my dad's horses and also kidnapped a woman. Then he was caught with this woman, running away; they caught him around here in Albuquerque. That's where they apprehended him. He was arrested for previous robberies as well as disturbances which he had committed. Very well then. This man had a family. And the woman when they caught him she returned to Cabezón. The horses which he had stolen from my grandfather, he had sold them in the Belen area. Ruperto Gonzales was arrested and taken to the penitentiary.

Later on Ruperto Gonzales escaped. When he did so, he ended up where his family was. He had two sons: one was Varisto and the other Antonio. This man spent a lot of time fleeing. My dad was already working in La Sierra (The Mountain), herding sheep. You've heard of El Ojo del Chatino (Flat Nose Spring), haven't you? That's where he was.

My dad said that Ruperto Gonzales would come for a drink of water and to give his horse some there at El Ojo del Chatino. He was running away from the authorities on a little white horse. Well, they didn't find him where his family was. He came and went, I guess. He'd come from time to time at night to where his wife was. His wife's name was Juanita. He kept on his toes, and my dad said that whenever the campsite was left unattended, Ruperto Gonzales would take food. He'd steal food from the camp. Evidently he'd go sleep at the volcanoes. That's where he'd hobble his horse, in a place where he couldn't be spotted, but my dad said he could spot him from the hillside as he (Ruperto Gonzales) approached the spring to drink water. He was constantly on his toes, until he left because someone informed the authorities that he had come for and taken his wife and the two boys. I believe that judging from the way in which he was headed, he was on his way to Arizona.

There's a lake called La Laguna del León (The Lion's Lake). At that time there was the mounted police. Those belonging to the mounted police had with them a man named El Pájaro (The Bird), and they were taking a siesta at La Laguna del León, by way of La Gaváchica. This Ruperto Gonzales had already hit the road on a horse wagon. His wife was driving. He took off running when the mounted police arrived in his pursuit. He jumped on his horse; he didn't take his rifle with him. He jumped on his horse and took off running and run he did, which is when they captured his family.

From La Laguna del León the mounted police returned to a ranch. Here there was a house close to the late Rudolfo Tachías's ranch. They put Ruperto Gonzales's wife inside the house, and they spread out their bedding in the patio in order to keep an eye on her. She huddled up inside the house with her two little boys. But this man, her husband, came back that night and showed up where his wife was. She fed him supper through the window. Then he said to her: "I'm going to give myself up. I'm tired of running," he supposedly said to her. His wife talked about that.

In any case, Ruperto Gonzales took off again, but, before doing so, he said to his wife: "If you can—because his rifle was still in the wagon—if you can, at La Angostura (The Strait)," there's a place called La Angostura, on the way back from Arroyo del Chico, on the other side of Don Donaciano's ranch, "if you can, you toss me my rifle from the wagon." For some reason she wasn't his yet, it was called La Vega de Marcos (Marcos's Pasture-lands), that's where they took a siesta. That's where the mounted wasn't his yet, it was called La Vega de Marcos (Marcos's Grass-land), that's where they took a siesta. That's where the mounted police dismounted, according to my dad. And this Pájaro, whom I mentioned earlier, was head of the contingency group, you see? El Pájaro turned back and he had his rifle loaded. Right there in La Angostura he bumped into the late Ruperto. Well, Ruperto recognized him and put up his arms, which is when El Pájaro put a bullet through his heart. The late Ruperto wasn't carrying a rifle. They even composed a ballad about him. I heard it in Cabezón. It went like this—what I can remember of it:

> El Pájaro ran into me at La Angostura,
> Made me put up my arms,
> And shot me through the heart.

Right near there, where his wife and sons were traveling, one of the sons, Antonio, is to have remarked: "They have killed my dad," because they heard the shot. As I say, it wasn't far.

And sure enough! El Pájaro came back and reported that he had killed him. Ruperto's wife burst out crying right away.

My wife's aunt who's already dead, she used to tell me about this man, Tomás Valencia, who was present at Ruperto Gonzales's wake. He saw the bullet hole, right smack in the heart.

La muerte de Juan Valdez

Bencés Gabaldón

Este hombre, era en mayo, pienso que era el día ocho de mayo, cuando lo mataron. No estaba grande yo, pero ya estaba . . . güeno, yo ya comprendía todo. Tendría como doce años o trece por ai. Este hombre lo mataron nomás porque él sabía que este Emiliano Sandoval había robao la estafeta. Éste tenía y faltaba dinero de la estafeta. Este hombre que mataron, él sabía quién se había llevao la estafeta. Y luego este Emiliano Sandoval pensó que aquel hombre lo iba a reportar al gobierno porque había robao la estafeta, pero él no había propuesto nada.

Este hombre, Juan Valdez, había andao todo el día buscando las bestias y llegó muy cansao y se acostó él con los hijos. Tenía tres hijos y se acostó él. Muy cansao y ai dormido le dieron unos hachazos. Le quebraron la cabeza. Uno le dio él, este Emiliano; él le dio primero. Y luego este otro Conrao, Conrao se llamaba, Conrao, pero no me puedo acordar de qué era. Era de por ai de Gualupe, de por ai era él. Él le dio el otro hachazo.

Y luego lo que hicieron jueron y lo sacaron arrastrando en peloto conforme estaba en la cama. Lo sacaron arrastrando y lo tiraron en un arroyo en la esquina del corral. Estaba cerquita. Lo sacaron y lo echaron en el arroyo. Estaba alto quizás y jueron y lo enterraron.

Pues de ai no puedo saber qué hicieron con él más. Lo que sé es que anduvieron en cortes y toitito eso pero no probaron nada porque los muchachos . . . uno de los hijos estaba hombre pero porque estaba juera de mente, poco juera de mente, no le agarraron de herencia; y los otros estaban chiquitos. No los agarraron porque eran de menor de edá.

Y luego, en poco tiempo, este Conrao se jue secando. Él no podía comer; él no podía beber agua. No podía hacer nada. Y luego le pegó una diarrea que se lo llevó; así se murió. Asina.

Y Emiliano se jue pa El Paso. Allá en El Paso salió su hijo en el carro y loo salió a matarse. Salió y le pegó a un poste de la luz. Y se quebró la cabeza el muchacho. Ai se acabó. Ai se acabó todo. Pagó el muchacho por él.

¿Ves? Pa que veigas tú lo que son las cosas. ¡Si naide se va de este mundo sin pagar las que debe!

The Death Of Juan Valdez

Bencés Gabaldón

This man, it was in May, I believe it was on the eighth of May, when he was murdered. I wasn't very old, but I was already . . . let me put it this way, I already knew the difference between right and wrong. I must have been about twelve or thirteen years old, or thereabouts. The only reason this man was murdered is because he knew that this fellow by the name of Emiliano Sandoval had robbed the post office. This fellow ran the post office and one day money was missing from it. The other man, the one who was murdered, he knew who had robbed the post office. Then this Emiliano Sandoval thought that the other man was going to turn him in to the authorities because he had robbed the post office, but the victim had never suggested any such thing.

This man was Juan Valdez, who had spent all day looking for his horses. He got home, very tired, and went to bed with his children. He had three children; he was a widower. He went to bed quite tired and there where he was sleeping received several blows with an axe. They busted up his head. This fellow Emiliano delivered one blow; he hit him first. And then this other guy Conrao, that was his name, but I don't recall his last name, he hailed from around Guadalupe, that's where he was from, he delivered the final blow with the axe.

And then what they did was to drag him naked, just the way he was in bed. They dragged him out and dumped him in an arroyo that ran by the corner of a corral. The place was close by. They took him out and dumped him in the arroyo. I guess the arroyo was deep enough so they went and buried him.

From then on I can't say what else they did. What I do know is that they (Emiliano and Conrao) went to trial and all of that, but nothing was proven because the children . . . one of the sons was already a grown man, but, because he was mentally retarded, a bit mentally retarded, his testimony was not admitted as evidence. And the other children were very small. Their testimony was not accepted because they were minors.

Then, within time, this fellow named Conrao began to wither away. He couldn't eat; he couldn't drink water. He couldn't do anything. And then he was stricken with a terrible diarrhea that marked the end of him; that's how he died. That's the way it was.

As for Emiliano, he went to El Paso. It was in El Paso that his son went out and killed himself in his car. He went out and hit a light post. And he busted his head, this fellow did. That was the end of him. That was the end of everything. The son paid for his father's wrongdoings.

See? See what things are like. No one departs from this earth without paying his debts!

La muerte de Juan Valdez

Nasario P. García

Te voy a contar de la muerte del dijunto Juan Valdez del Cabezón. Éste, el dijunto Juan Valdez, era hombre solo. Le quedaron dos de familia. Había Avelino, que le decían, era el más grande. Y la muchachita, estaba chiquita. Ella no supo nada pero este Avelino sí. Es que vido todo. Él estaba medio tonto. Pues habían entrao dos una noche, con una vela, o con un farol, pero más bien con una vela. Y onde estaba durmiendo le dieron con una hacha. De ai lo sacaron, lo sacaron arrastrando con un caballo, de la casa. Había un arroyo que corría cerca de la casa, y lo sacaron y lo tiraron en ese arroyo. ¿Y sabes tú dónde estaba esa casa? ¿Tú sabes ónde abaja uno La Cuesta de Chihuahua, cuando ya plana uno, pa aquel lao del Río Puerco, pa aquel lao asina? Ai vivía el dijunto Juan Valdez. Al otro lao del río, pal lao de la placita de Cabezón. Yo creo que toavía ora se notarán ruinas de la casa. Agarraron a los que lo mataron, porque Avelino los entregó. Él supo quiénes jueron. ¿Quién sabe por qué lo mataron?

Yo no estaba nacido toavía. Nomás oía pláticas de hombres grandes cuando andábanos ai por todo ese pais.

The Death Of Juan Valdez

Nasario P. García

I'm going to tell you about the death of the late Juan Valdez from Cabezón. The late Juan Valdez was a widower. He was left with two children. There was Avelino, as he was called. He was the older. And the little girl; she was very small. She didn't know what happened but Avelino did. He presumably saw everything, but he was a bit off his rocker. Well, two men with a candle entered his house one night, or perhaps it was a lantern, but more than likely it was a candle. Right there where he was sleeping they struck him with an axe. From there they took him out, they dragged him out of the house. There was an arroyo that ran close to the house, and they dumped him in it. And do you know where that house was? Do you know where the Cuesta de Chihuahua (Chihuahua Slope) is, after you get to the bottom of the slope, toward the other side of the Río Puerco? That's where the late Juan Valdez lived. On the other side of the road, on the side where the village of Cabezón is located. I believe the ruins of the house are still visible today.

They caught the men who murdered him because Avelino turned them in. He knew who they were. Who knows why they killed him?

I wasn't born yet. I only heard bits and pieces from older men when we roamed that part of the country.

3

Their Religion

Nothing played a more important role in the daily lives of Río Puerco Valley residents than religion. Children were not allowed to sit at the dinner table without saying grace both before and after eating. At night they knelt by their bedsides and said prayers before going to bed; in the morning they knelt again and thanked God for seeing the light of day once more. Faith that God knows all was unwavering, as is shown in the story, "The Catholic Cows."

Religion was a very personal matter, and the people felt an intimate footing with the saints, or santos. This is perhaps best illustrated in the story told me by Susanita Ramírez de Armijo, "Punishing the Santos," and again in "The Baby Jesus" and "Parading a Santo." Everyone, from a very young age, had his favorite santo, such as Luciano Sánchez's, El Santo Niño de Atocha. This was one of the most favored of the santos in Guadalupe. Some people had more than one santo to whom they directed their prayers in time of grief or duress. La Virgen de Guadalupe, the patron saint, was obviously a popular one in Guadalupe. Neighboring communities had their own favorite santos.

Even in religion, a stoic cynicism, acceptance of things as they are, is sometimes apparent, as in Adelita Gonzales's remembrances about her grandfather's teachings, "When God is Unwilling, Santos are Helpless."

There were, of course, unique individuals like "The Healer," who seemed to be a holy man. He, unlike other strangers or outsiders who ventured to the Río Puerco Valley, was apparently looked upon favorably by people of the San Luis community. The penitentes, also referred to as *hermanos* or laybrothers, commanded respect in their community. They were known, among other things, for celebrating Ash Wednesday by praying and beating themselves with whips in the graveyard after midnight. In the absence of a permanent priest, however, people often relied on the penitentes for spiritual guidance and inspiration. The relationship between both parties was, to a large extent good, regardless of whether some individuals accepted or even completely understood the principles espoused by the penitentes.

Religion was also a community affair, especially during Lent, Holy Week, Christmas, and Epiphany. Baptismals, wakes (*velorios*), and weddings involved virtually every member of the community as well as neighbors from surrounding areas. Religious processions were popular in the summer. The local patron saint was paraded throughout the village, going from house to house, where each family paid homage, until the santo was returned to the church a few days later.

In brief, even though the priest came to celebrate Mass in Guadalupe and each of the other villages only once a month, people faithfully practiced their religion. On special saint's days, they suspended all work, as they also did on Sunday. Religion was an integral part of their daily lives, a part of the innermost being of the people who lived in the Río Puerco Valley, and remained so until death.

Las vacas católicas

Susanita Ramírez de Armijo

Como allá en Gualupe no había misa todos los domingos, mi agüelo tenía una costumbre. Nos juntábanos todos los nietos y teníanos de rezar el rosario en la mañana, en el domingo, junto con él. Y loo que ya rezábanos el rosario, nos llevaba él pa esta cochera muy grandota que tenía él. Y tenía una viga grandota en el medio y ai nos sentaba. Y ai nos dicía lo que iba a venir en este mundo, y lo que iba a pasar, como que iban a venir los trenes, los carros. Él nos platicaba todo eso. "Ya yo no lo voy a ver," dicía, "pero ustedes sí."

Platicaba de los oroplanos que iban a venir a volar. ¡Todo eso!

Y tamién nos dicía: "Miren. Siempre cuando ustedes oigan bramar las vacas que se arrodillan en el llano, es que va a pasar algo en este mundo."

Las vacas se arrodillaban en estos tiempos, según los viejos. Estaban muy católicas las vacas porque si iba a pasar alguna cosa se ponían de rodillas.

Y de ai lo creí yo a mi agüelo porque una vez íbanos de Gualupe, como pal rumbo de Cebolleta, mi *daddy*, yo y mi mamá. Tendría yo unos doce años yo creo, y oímos una música, y loo vimos que las vacas se arrodillaron. Y dijo mi *daddy*:

—¡Miren lo que va a suceder!

Pus paró mi *daddy* los caballos y juimos a ver y nada. Como a los tres meses o algo así, se mataron mis hermanos. Había una seña quizás que ya Dios le mandaba a mi *daddy*.

Pero los viejos, muy viejos, de antes, sabían todo eso. Estaba todo a su cabeza. No tenían educación pero los hombres como mi agüelo nos contaban muncho. Mi agüelo tenía un libro que le llamaba El Archivo. Era una biblia. Era un libro alto. Y de ai nos leía él muncho.

The Catholic Cows

Susanita Ramírez de Armijo

In Guadalupe, since Mass was not celebrated every Sunday, my grandfather had a custom. Every Sunday morning all of the grandchildren got together, and we had to say the rosary right along with him. And then once we said the rosary, he'd take us to this really huge barn that he had. There right in the middle of it was a large beam and that's where he sat us. It was there that he'd tell us the things that were going to come into this world, such as trains and cars. He used to tell us all of that. "I'm not going to see them," he'd say, "but you're going to."

He spoke about the airplanes that would some day make their mark on the skies. He'd tell us all of that!

And he would also say to us: "Look. Anytime you hear cows bellowing and kneeling on the plains, that's a bad omen."

You see, according to the old-timers, back in those days cows used to kneel on the plains. The cows were good Catholics because if something terrible was forthcoming, they'd kneel down.

From then on I believed whatever my grandfather said. One time we were headed for Cebolleta from Guadalupe—my daddy, my mom and I. I guess I must have been about twelve years old, and we heard some music playing; then we noticed the cows kneeling down. And my daddy said:

"Look! Something's going to happen."

So my daddy stopped the horses, and we went to see and sure enough! In about three months or so, my two brothers were killed. There was like a signal that God was already communicating to him.*

But the old-timers, the very old ones from way back, they knew all about that sort of thing. Everything was at their finger

*These are the two boys who were killed when the river bank fell on them, p. 83.

tips. True, they didn't have a formal education, but old-timers like my grandfather would tell us many things. He had a book he used to call The Archive. It was his bible; it was a tall book. And that's where he read a lot to us from.

El castigar a los santos

Susanita Ramírez de Armijo

Pus la gente tapaba a los santos con un velo negro y los ponía ai por tanto tiempo porque estaban castigaos.

Yo me acuerdo que mi mamá castigaba a la Virgen. Esta virgen que ella tenía iban de todo el lugar de Gualupe a visitala. Se llamaba Santa Bárbara. Y cuando la tenía castigada la tenía en un nicho y allá estaba volteada pa la pader y tapada. Naiden la vía. La castigaba por alguna razón, quizás por alguna roga que tenía o no sé qué, pero siempre castigaba mi mamá a su santo. Ai tenía que estar tapada la Virgen hasta que ya cumplía la penitencia que le daba mamá.

Como cuando hacían velorio. Yo me acuerdo una vez que mi hermano y mi compadre Carpio se robaron a San Antonio en la mitá de la noche. Se lo llevaron muy lejos. Pus jueron todos a buscalo; la misma noche lo jueron a buscar. Lo encontraron, pero no jue hasta la madrugada. En la madrugada ya trujieron a San Antonio, yo me acuerdo, y vino toda la gente que estaba en el velorio. A ellos, a mi hermano y a mi compadre Carpio, a ellos los amarraron atrás del carro de bestias y los llevaron a casa. Ai iban castigaos junto con el santo. Otro día tuvieron que estar hincaos todo el día en lao del altar pa que pagaran el castigo que les dieron porque se habían robao a San Antonio.

Otra vez me acuerdo yo que se perdió un caballo de nosotros, un caballo muy consentido que teníanos nosotros en el rancho. Entre todos juimos cantando un alabao, con amá y mis hermanos, pallá pa un lugar que le llamábanos El Rincón. Allá abajo de una piedra dejamos el santo. Ai lo tapamos; ai lo dejamos.

Sereno le llamábanos a ese caballo. Se perdió y no lo jallábanos. Y loo más tarde vino el caballo solo; antonces vino el caballo pero solo. Y loo juimos otra vez cantando alabaos y velamos ai en casa al santo porque trujo al caballo.

Punishing The Santos

Susanita Ramírez de Armijo

People in Guadalupe used to cover the santos with a veil of black gauze and place them in a certain spot for a period of time because they were being punished.

I remember my mother punishing the Virgin. Everyone from Guadalupe used to pay their respects to this Virgin that my mother had. Her name was Santa Barbara. Whenever my mother punished her, she placed it in a niche, and that's where it remained—covered and facing the wall. Nobody could see her. My mom had her reasons for punishing her. Perhaps it was due to a religious vow, or something like that, but she always punished her favorite santo. The Virgin had to remain covered until she fulfilled whatever penance my mom would impose upon her.

Take, for instance, a religious wake. I recall that on one occasion a brother of mine and my compadre Carpio, right in the middle of the night, stole the santo of Saint Anthony. They took him far away. That very same night, everyone went searching for it. It was already in the wee hours of the morning when he was returned. That I remember. And all of the people who had been at the wake came back. My brother and my compadre Carpio were tied to the back of a horse wagon and taken back home. They were being punished right along with Saint Anthony. On the following day, my brother and compadre had to spend the entire day on their knees next to the church altar in retribution for having stolen the santo of Saint Anthony.

On another occasion—it comes to mind—a horse of ours, a very favorite horse that we had on the ranch, got lost. All of us, including my mom and my brothers, headed for a place we referred to as El Rincón (The Corner). As we marched along, all of us in unison sang a religious hymn of praise. When we reached our destination, that's where we left this certain santo, right under a rock, after covering it up.

Sereno, that's what we called the horse. He got lost and we couldn't find him. Then much later the horse returned by itself; that's when he showed up. Alone. Then once again the singing of religious hymns of praise was repeated, plus we had another wake at home in honor of the religious statue for having returned our horse.

El sacar del santo

Adrián Chávez

En esos años pasaos se observaba el sacar del santo, a donde-
quiera. Pues tocó que en un pueblo de indios, sacaron al Santo
Niño pa que lloviera porque estaba muy seco. Como al tercer día
que lo sacaron, empezó a llover muncho, que hasta tuvieron que
dejar al Santo Niño por allí en una casa porque la lluvia era
muncha. Empezaron a bajar las cañadas llenas de agua; hicieron
destrozo y todo. Bueno, pues, terminó la procesión del Santo
Niño y lo rezaron.

Decidieron los otros indios grandes de sacar tamién a la Virgen
pa dale gracias a Dios, de ver que había llovido y todo eso. Tocó
que el último día que ya venían con la Virgen patrás, este indio
viejo les dijo que pararan poquito pa rezar él tamién. Fue, pasó
pa delante, y se hincó, delante de la Virgen. Pero con muncha fe
él. Estaba rezando y le dice:

—¿Sabes Virgencita Milagrosa por qué te traemos por aquí?
¡Porque mires la cagada que hizo tu hijo!

Parading a Santo

Adrián Chávez

Back in those years the parading of a santo was observed everywhere. It so happened that in an Indian village, they took out the Baby Jesus for it to rain because it was very dry. On about the third day of taking out the santo, it started to rain, so much so that the people had to leave the Baby Jesus in one of the homes because the rain was quite heavy. The cañadas full of water started to run; they caused a lot of destruction and all. Well, then, the procession for the Baby Jesus ended. They prayed to Him.

The rest of the older Indians decided to take out the Virgin in a similar procession so as to express their appreciation to God, since it had rained and all. It so happened that on the last day that they were returning with the Virgin, this old Indian told them to stop for a little bit in order for him to pray also. He went to the front and knelt down in front of the Virgin, but with a lot of faith. He was praying and he said to her:

"Do you know my Miraculous Little Virgin why we've got You out here? So that you see the crappy mess your son made!"

El Santo Niño de Atocha

Luciano Sánchez

El Santo Niño de Atocha conmigo ha sido muy popular. Cuando yo me requié, yo lo traiba asina en mi bolsa. Cuando jui al espital que me pusieron, que me arreglaron la boca, yo estaba peleao con él en la mañana, porque lo había mostrao, que lo había mostrao yo en la sierra, montes, arroyos y too. Pues ya cuando él se quería ir del espital, le teníanos yo y mi vieja una sábana. No, pues yo lo agarraba de aquí de los brazos en medio del cuarto, y de aquí brincaba pa la sábana. Él quería irse solo y yo quería llevalo. Pos otro día que amanecí llegó mi vieja y le digo yo:

—¿Sabes tú que me peleé con el Santo Niño? Él quería irse y yo no quería que se juera. Yo quería llevalo.

—Sí—dijo—. Allá lo tengo en la casa. Nomás sales de aquí, del espital, y te lo voy a dar.

Pues llegó del espital a mi casa. Ai lo cuidó mi vieja hasta que saliera yo. El Santo Niño de Atocha ya estaba más apurao que yo.

The Holy Child Of Atocha

Luciano Sánchez

The Holy Child of Atocha has been one of my favorites. When I got into a wreck, I had Him in my hip pocket. When I went to the hospital, where they patched my mouth all up, He was crossed with me in the morning, all because I had carried Him around with me to the sierra, mountains, arroyos, and so forth. When He was ready to leave the hospital, my wife and I had a bed sheet for Him to be wrapped up in. There you are, why I'd grab Him by the arms in the middle of the room, and from there He'd jump to the bed sheet. He wanted to leave alone and I wanted to take Him myself. Next day when I woke up my wife showed up and I say to her:

"Do you know that I got in a fight with the Holy Child? He wanted to leave and I didn't want Him to do so. I wanted to take Him myself."

"Yes," she said. "I have Him at home. As soon as you leave the hospital, I'm going to let you have Him."

Well He went from the hospital to the house. My wife took care of Him there until I left the hospital. The Holy Child of Atocha was in more of a hurry than I was.

El Santo Niño

Bencés Gabaldón

A unos tíos míos los cautivaron los indios de Pánana. Y cuando a ellos los cautivaron estos indios, se los llevaron. Ellos, mis tíos, andaban cuidando borregas. Estaban chiquitos, y se los llevaron los indios de Pánana. Eran tres mis tíos. Y luego los dividieron en los pueblos porque eran siete pueblos. Uno en un pueblo y los otros en otros; los separaron. Y se estuvieron cinco años ellos allá; los tuvieron cautivos por cinco años.

Antonces jue el gobierno y hizo lucha por ellos pa ver si los sacaba de aá. Antonces su mamá de mi tío Rafel, uno de los cautivos, jue y cautivó al Santo Niño. Hizo un nicho, en la pader. Y luego metió al Santo Niño. Y lo tuvo cautivo. Cuando ya dieron en dicho que estaban mis tíos en los pueblos de Pánana y el gobierno los iba a sacar, que ya tuvieron en dicho que los iban a sacar, entonces empezó el Santo Niño a tocar la pader. Cuando ya los sacaron, es que tiró el Santo Niño la pader y cayó, porque ya los habían sacao a mis tíos. ¿Ves? Y los trujieron; los trujieron pacá. Y antonces se los entregaron a los papaces.

The Baby Jesus

Bencés Gabaldón

Several uncles of mine were captured once by the Pawnee Indians. And when they captured them, they took them away. My uncles were herding sheep at the time. They were quite small, but the Pawnee Indians took them anyway. There were three uncles. The Indians then split them among the pueblos, because there were seven pueblos. One in one pueblo and the others in another, they were separated. And my uncles stayed captured for five years; they were kept captive for five years.

It was then that the government did something in their behalf to see if it could set them free. Then my uncle Ralph's mother, he being one of the captives, went and captured the Baby Jesus. She carved out a niche in the wall, where she later put Him. She plastered over the Baby Jesus and held Him captive. When the word got around that my uncles were being held captive by the Pawnee Indians, and that the government was going to free them, that it for sure was going to get them out, then the Baby Jesus began knocking on the wall from the inside. When my uncles were finally set free, I understand that Baby Jesus knocked the wall down and fell over, an indication that my uncles had been let go. You see? And they were returned; they were returned to San Luis. They were handed over to their parents.

El milagro del Santo Niño de Atocha

Edumenio Lovato

Candelaria, la hermana de Rafael, era dueña orgullosa de un santo pequeño, el Santo Niño de Atocha. Desde niña había guardado una devoción ardiente para con el Santo Niño, siguiendo el ejemplo de su madre, que también era una devota fiel del Santo Niño. Todos los días en sus rezos no se le olvidaba rezarle al Niño Jesús para la protección cotidiana de su familia. Ella poseía una fe intensa desde niña para con el Santo Niño de Atocha.

Cuando Candelaria supo que su hermano Rafael había sido capturado y que los indios se lo habían llevado le dio un susto. Ella amaba mucho a Rafaelito. Por días ella lo echó de menos. Su hermano siempre estaba en sus pensamientos. Lo único que podía hacer para ayudarle era rezar por él. Día tras día en sus oraciones le suplicaba al Santo Niño que librara a su hermano de su cautiverio y que lo trajera a casa.

Había una costumbre entre la gente hispana en esos días, especialmente entre las mujeres que eran devotas fervorosas del Santo Niño de Atocha, y quienes durante tiempos de desgracia en sus vidas encerraban al Santo Niño. Esto se hacía por esconder o poner al Santo Niño en un lugar no muy obvio y tenerlo escondido, mientras rezaban y guardaban la esperanza que el Santo Niño les otorgara su pedido. Todo esto se hacía durante períodos de crisis en sus vidas.

Candelaria estaba muy al tanto de esta costumbre. Ella creía firmemente que el Santo Niño salvaría a su hermano Rafael y que lo devolvería a su casa. Aunque ella rezaba todos los días por su hermano, decidió hacer algo más atrevido para conseguir lo que ella quería. Ella encarceló al Santo Niño.

Una de las paredes de adentro del cuarto donde ella decía sus oraciones, Candelaria hizo un nicho, bastante grande y profundo para que cupiera el santo pequeño, el Santo Niño. Antes de que pusiera al santo dentro del nicho, ella, en su actitud infantil, le advirtió al Santo Niño que lo iba a tener preso hasta que Él trajera a casa a su hermano Rafael—y salvo. Entonces ella colocó al pequeño santo dentro del nicho y cerró la apertura enjarrándola con zoquete.

Se pasaron semanas, meses y años, pero Candelaria munca dejó de hacer sus ruegos diarios al Santo Niño para que devolviera a su hermano. Un día, al acercarse el quinto aniversario del cautiverio de Rafael, mientras ella estaba absorta en sus oraciones cerca de su altarcito, oyó un golpe, como si alguien estuviera a la puerta. Ella fue a la puerta pero no había nadie. A la noche siguiente mientras estaba rezando, volvió a oír un toque y otra vez fue a la puerta pero no había nadie. Lo mismo ocurrió la tercera noche, pero esta vez Candelaria se dio cuenta que el golpe venía desde adentro del nicho. "¿Qué significaría éste?," se preguntó. Se acostó esa noche pensando en ello. A la mañana siguiente, temprano, ella entró en el cuarto y, al hacerlo, lo primero que notó fue el enjarre en el suelo. Al instante vio hacia arriba del nicho y se quedó asombrada de ver lo que vio. ¡El Santo Niño estaba en plena vista! ¡El nicho estaba abierto! En aquel instante Candelaria sabía, dentro de su corazón, que su hermano Rafael había sido rescatado y que lo vería dentro de poco. El Santo Niño por fin le había hecho caso a sus ruegos y al fin le había concedido su pedido. ¡El Santo Niño de Atocha había desempeñado un milagro! Unos días más tarde volvió Rafael de su cautiverio.

Rafael Lovato llegó a ser hombre, y uno de los primeros para establecerse en el Río Puerco. Los primeros pobladores nombraron su aldeíta La Tijera, Nuevo México. Más tarde le renombraron San Luis. Rafael solicitó una heredad y llegó a una edad bien vieja. Cuando murió fue sepultado en el campo santo cerca de la primera iglesia que construyeron los primeros pobladores de La Tijera. Al morir, Rafael todavía tenía señas de su cautiverio: dos agujeritos, uno en cada perilla de la oreja.

La hermana de Rafael, Candelaria, se casó con uno de la familia Domínguez, y se pasó el resto de su vida en La Tijera. Cuando murió, a ella también la enterraron en el primer campo santo de La Tijera.

The Miracle Of The Holy Child Of Atocha

Edumenio Lovato

Rafael's sister, Candelaria, was a proud possessor of a small santo of the Holy Child of Atocha. From childhood she had maintained an ardent devotion for the Holy Child, following the example of her mother who was also a faithful devotee of the Holy Child. Every day in her prayers Candelaria never forgot to pray to the Child Jesus for the daily protection of her family. She possessed an intense child-like faith in the Holy Child of Atocha.

When Candelaria learned that her brother Rafael had been captured and carried away by the Indians, she was shocked. She loved Rafaelito very much. For days she grieved for him. Her brother was always in her thoughts. The only thing she could do to help her brother was to pray for him. Day after day in her daily prayers she pleaded with the Holy Child to save her brother from his captivity and bring him home.

There was a custom among Hispanic people in those days, especially among women who were zealous devotees of the Holy Child of Atocha, and who when in time of adversity in their lives would place the Holy Child in captivity. This was done by hiding or placing the Holy Child statue in an inconspicuous place and keeping the santo in hiding, praying and hoping that the Holy Child would grant them their requests. This was done mostly in time of a great calamity in their lives.

Candelaria was well versed on this custom. She firmly believed that the Holy Child would save her brother Rafael and bring him home. Though she prayed daily for her brother, she decided to take a more drastic measure to ensure the granting of her request. She placed the Holy Child in captivity.

On one of the inside walls of the room where she said her daily prayers, Candelaria dug out a small niche, large enough and deep enough for the small santo of the Holy Child to fit in. Before she placed the santo inside the niche, in her child-like attitude, admonished the Holy Child that she was going to keep Him a prisoner until He would bring her brother Rafael home and safe. She then placed the small santo inside the niche and closed the opening by plastering it with mud.

Weeks, months, and years passed but Candelaria never ceased her daily pleadings to the Holy Child for her brother's return. One day, near the fifth anniversary of Rafael's captivity, while she was absorbed in her evening prayers near her small altar, she heard a knock, as if someone was at the door. She went to the door but found no one there. The following evening while praying, again she heard a knock and again went to the door but found no one. It happened again the third evening, but this time Candelaria realized that the knocking was coming from inside the niche. "What could it mean," she wondered? She retired that night thinking about it. Early the next morning she went into the room and as she stepped inside, the first thing she noticed was the crumbled plaster on the floor. Instantly she looked up at the niche and gasped in amazement at the sight before her. The Holy Child was in full view! The niche was open! At that moment Candelaria knew, deep in her heart, that her brother Rafael had been rescued and would see him soon. The Holy Child had finally listened to her pleadings and had at last granted her request. The Holy Child of Atocha had performed a miracle! A few days later Rafael returned home from his captivity.

Rafael Lobato grew to manhood, and was one of the first to settle on the Río Puerco. The first settlers named their small town La Tijera, later on renamed San Luis, New Mexico. Rafael applied for a homestead and lived to a ripe old age. When he died he was buried in the cemetery near the first church the first settlers of La Tijera had built. At death, Rafael still carried marks of his captivity, two small holes, one on each ear lobe.

Rafael's sister, Candelaria, married into a Domínguez family, and spent the rest of her life in La Tijera. When she died, she, too, was buried in the first cemetery at La Tijera.

El Sanador

Salomón Lovato

Mi agüelita y todos yo creo, todas las gentes, rezaban el rosario, antes de acostarse. O se convidaban unos a los otros a rezar el rosario. A lo menos en mi lugar mío. Yo no sé pallá pa Gualupe y esos lugares. Yo creo que todo era la misma cosa. De todos modos, estaba un señor que vino en el mil novecientos . . . yo estaba muy chiquito, puede que tuviera como unos tres o cuatro años. Vino un hombre que le decían El Sanador. Andaba . . . traiba el cabello lo mismo que Cristo y andaba vestido lo mismo que Cristo. Traiba un caballo moro y una silla nueva. Y yo me acuerdo ver la gente que decía: "Va venir El Sanador," sanador quería decir *healer*.

Y jue pa San Luis, y mi hermano el mayor, él estaba tullido cuando era un muchachito. Yo lo vide al hombre este. Pero él jue a cierta casa y ai estaba. Traiba, como digo, un caballo moro grandote él, y le quitaba la silla y lo soltaba y luego rezaba y procuraba sanar a la gente. Y le daban de comer y too eso, pero le daban dinero y no lo agarraba. Antonces se iba de un lugar a otro.

Yo tenía un retrato de él pero no sé qué diablos pasó con él. Se perdió. Eso es algo que siempre me ha apenao porque se parecía la misma cosa de Cristo, la misma cosa de Cristo. Un hombre muy bonito. No sé si tu papá se acuerda de eso, si se acuerda de El Sanador.

The Healer

Salomón Lovato

My grandma and everybody else, I believe, all of the people, said the rosary, before going to bed. Or they invited one another to say the rosary. At least in my village they did. I don't know about over in Guadalupe and those places. I believe it was the same all over. In any case, there was a man who came in nineteen hundred . . . I was very small. Maybe I was about three or four years old. A man came who was called The Healer. He wore his hair just like Christ and was dressed like Him too. He had a blue-gray horse and a new saddle. And I remember the people saying: "The Healer's going to come."

And he went to San Luis and my brother, the eldest, was paralyzed when he was a little boy. I saw this man. But he went to a certain home and there he was. He had, as I said, a huge blue-gray horse. He'd take off its saddle, turn it loose; then he'd pray and try to cure the people. They'd feed him and all of that, and they'd give him money but he wouldn't accept it. Then he went from one place to another.

I had a picture of him but I don't know what in the devil happened to it. It got lost. Something that's bothered me all the time is that he resembled Christ so much, the same thing as Christ. A very handsome man. I don't know if your father remembers that, whether he recalls the Healer.

Cuando Dios no quiere, santos no pueden

Adelita Gonzales

Decían munchas veces que andaban ai con los santos a los troteros. Le pedía alguno al santo un milagro y le decía: "¡A ver si
me dejan ir al baile esta noche! Si no me dejan te voy a castigar;
mañana te voy a castigar."

Si no lo dejaban a uno ir al baile, pues aquí anda uno con
aquel pobre santo castigándolo. ¡Pues qué culpa tenía el pobre
santo! Y había veces que el santo quizá les movía la conciencia a
los padres y dejaban ir a las hijas al baile. ¡Oh! Otro día venían a
prendele velas al santo.

Yo nunca los castigué. Yo no sé. A mí me enseñó mi
agüelito—no era mi agüelito—le decíanos agüelito. Él era tío.
Pero le contemplábanos como mi papá Toribio Salas. Yo de muy
chiquita, de diez años, sabía ler mejicano, porque él me en-
señaba. Y me enseañaba muncho de rezar. Yo rezaba el rosario.
Me decía:

—Nunca castigues a los santos mi hijita. Si quieres, pídeles y
diles que te concedan.

Y sí. Yo agarraba el Sagrao de Corazón de Jesús: "Ayúdame en
estas mis necesidades. O María Santísima que me ayudes en lo
que te pido. Si me conviene y si no que te haga tu santo agrado,"
les decía.

Eso me enseñó mi agüelito. Siempre decía:

—No los castigues mi hijita porque "cuando Dios no quiere,
santos no pueden."

Cuando Dios no quiere dale el privilegio al santo pa que lo
haga (el milagro), no lo castigues a él porque él ha hecho su
juerza. Él ha hecho su juerza. Pero si Dios no quiere, no te con-
cede el milagro. Pero pídele con todo tu corazón, decía.

Y asina quedé impuesta yo. Yo les pido mis devotos al Sagrao Corazón y a María Santísima, que es a los que traigo en los troteros. El Santo Niño es otro. Ésos son mis santos favoritos.

When God's Unwilling, Santos Are Helpless

Adelita Gonzales

It was said many times that people went around like crazy with santos. Some individual would request some farfetched thing of a santo by saying something like: "Let's see if I get permission to go to the dance tonight! If I don't, I'm going to punish you."

Why if one did not get permission to go to a dance, here you are running hither and thither punishing that poor santo. Why was the poor santo to blame? There were times when the santo did in fact influence the parents and the girls received permission to attend the dance. Oh, you wouldn't believe it! Next day they'd light candles to the santo.

I never punished them. I don't know why. My grandfather taught me—he wasn't my grandfather, we just called him that. He was an uncle, but we treated him like a grandfather. From the time I was very small, about ten years old, I knew how to read Spanish, because he taught me. And he taught me a lot about praying. I said the rosary. He'd tell me:

"Never punish the santos, my dear child. If you wish, request things from them and ask them to grant them to you."

And that's what I'd do. I'd get ahold of the Sacred Heart of Jesus and say: "Help me in these predicaments. Please, oh Virgin Mother of God help me in this request of mine. If I deserve it, and it meets with your approval."

That's what my grandfather taught me. He always said:

"Don't punish them, my dear child, because 'When God's unwilling, santos are helpless.'"

Whenever God doesn't wish to grant a santo the privilege of carrying it (the miracle) out, don't punish the santo because He's done his part. He's done his part. But if God's unwilling, He won't grant you your miracle. But if you do ask for something, do so with all of your heart, my grandfather would say to me.

And that's the way I was brought up. I pray devoutly to the Sacred Heart and to the Holy Virgin; they are the ones I "carry around" in my comings-and-goings. The Holy Jesus is another one. Those are my favorite santos.

Los Penitentes

Adelita Gonzales

Pues desde que se empezaba el Miércoles de Ceniza, íbanos a rezar. Rezábanos las Estaciones, rezábanos en la noche el rosario,
junto con los Hermanos, los Penitentes que les llamaban más antes.

Pues ellos rezaban su rosario. Munchos—yo no los llegué a
ver—más antes decían que se desciplinaban muncho. Estos últimos años, sí víanos que ellos hacían sus penitencias después de
las doce de la noche. Iban a un campo santo pero ellos solos; iban
a hacer sus penitencias, sus oraciones o lo que jueran hacer ellos.
Desciplinarse, como decían, que se daban azotes y too eso. Yo no
llegé a ver eso.

Munchos no creiban en munchas de estas cosas; pues decían
que no les gustaba y no sé qué. Pero era una de las cosas que mi
Dios sufrió por nosotros. Jue una de las cosas que el Señor
padeció por nosotros.

Munchas veces aquí, eso sí llegué a ver yo, en San Luis, en casa
no lo hicieron, pero en San Luis sí llevaban tres muchachitos en la
cruz. Los amarraban, los ponían en la cruz. Uno era el Señor y los
otros eran los dos ladrones que le llaman. Ai "clavaban" a los
muchachitos; ai los tenían. Yo no sé, se me hace que todavía lo
hacen. Y cuando ya llegaba el tiempo de que los apeaban, ese
día, por el medio día, los abajaban de la cruz. Estos niños los
ponían como cierto modo pa que ellos estuvieran paraos. Hacían
la cruz y todo y loo pues, por ejemplo, les ponían una cosa para
que estuvieran sus piececitos agustos y luego con unos cabrestitos
los amarraban asina (con nudos) y ai estaban ellos. No los tenían
muncho tampoco; nomás lo que juera llegar a la estación. Antonces los bajaban.

The Penitentes

Adelita Gonzales

Well, from the time Ash Wednesday started, we went to pray. We said the Stations of the Cross, the rosary at night, along with the Brothers, the Penitentes as they were called long ago.

They said their own rosary. Many people—I never got to see the Brothers—long ago claimed that they disciplined themselves a lot. During these last few years, of course we saw that they complied with their penance after midnight. They'd go to a cemetery, but alone, to do their penance, say their prayers or whatever they went there for. To discipline themselves, according to some people, meant self-flagellation and all of that. I never saw that.

Many people didn't believe in some of those things; why they'd say that they didn't like them and what not. But self-flagellation was one of those things that symbolized what Christ suffered for us.

Many times there in San Luis, that I got to see myself, not at home in Guadalupe, but in San Luis, they used to carry three little boys on a cross. They were tied and put on the cross. One played the role of Christ and two other boys were the so-called thiefs. That's where they'd "nail" and keep the two little boys. I don't know, but it seems to me that they still practice that. And when it came time to lower them down, on the same day, about noon, they were taken off the cross. These kids were put on the cross in a certain way in order for them to be upright, like standing up. The cross and everything else would be erected and then, for example, something was on their feet so they would be comfortable before tying them down. The people didn't have the kids on the cross for long, only long enough to get to the station (Calvary). Then they were brought down.

4
Mischief

When I was growing up on a farm in Guadalupe, our usual nightly entertainment was to sit on the kitchen floor and listen to the adults tell stories as the kerosene lamp flickered. Sometimes it involved only my parents and grandparents (*agüelitos*, as they were called), but at other times relatives and friends would come, and then the stories and remembrances would flow. Their recollections were based on their own experiences and the tales they had heard when they were children. When the episodes had comical aspects, the storyteller would often exaggerate to keep the interest high. We children did not join into the conversation, but we listened and enjoyed hearing what was said.

The stories in this section all have comical aspects, though some with a bittersweet touch, as "A Very Mean Cow," "A Poor Little Old Indian," and "My Grandfathers." We see once more the cynical acceptances of things as they were in "I Lost by One Vote." Many, as "Drunks," "Kids," "Two Priests," and "The Rooster Race" while funny, illustrate the bravado of the young men, particularly when they were strutting before the girls.

"The Wake" illustrates the mischief of a small child, as well as his curiosity. The child undoubtedly convinced his mother to allow him to attend the *velorio* so as to witness first-hand what a religious wake was like. Once there, the peculiar noise which taunted him scared the wits out of him. This was the price he paid for being curious about religious wakes.

The story of the two astronomers is an old one, but it is a favorite of mine. In "Two Aspiring Young Astronomers," the burro, a beast of burden, is also looked upon as stupid, hence the unflattering use of burro to impugn a person's intellect. The donkey has the last laugh, as it were, because of his purported knowledge of the stars.

Mis agüelos

Salomón Lovato

Yo me acuerdo que mis dos agüelos vivieron con mi mamá, con nosotros, porque los dos estaban viudos. Nomás que mi agüelo por el lao de mamá, era más viejo que mi agüelo del lao de en papá. Pero ya estaban viejos. Mi agüelo por el lao de mi mamá se murió de ochenta y siete años. Y el otro se murió de ochenta y uno o algo así. De manera que ellos tuvieron munchas experiencias.

Pero ai estaban los viejitos. No había nada que hacer. Por el lao de en papá, él era muy astuto. Él tenía borregas; tenía dinero. Quedó viudo pero todo le quitaron las mujeres. Y el otro no, era pobre. Era sembrador, nomás. Le gustaba cortar un pedazo de madera con navaja, con la navaja. Pero él era poeta. Componía munchos versos y, y era un hombre muy sabio, muy inteligente, pero no tenía nada educación. De todos modos, él era murre miedoso. Por el lao de en papá, él no era, ah, no era miedoso. No tenía miedo. Hasta era muy travieso.

Güeno. Se ponían ellos los dos a platicar, de lo de antes. "Usté compadre," decía uno, "que usté no jue pa los Estaos. Yo sí jui. Llegué a pelear ai con los indios y usté no. Está aquí. Se crió aquí," le decía. Y le decía el otro: "Si yo me muero compadre primero que usté," le decía mi papá Ignacio, ése era el astuto, a mi padrecito Telesfor, a uno le decía yo en papá y al otro padrecito, "si yo me muero primero lo voy a venir agarrar de las patas."

Y mi padrecito Telesfor vivía como, oh, retiradito de la casa de nosotros. Muérese en papá Ignacio primero, el que le dijo que iba a venir, y mi padrecito Telesfor ya no quería vivir aá más solo.

My Grandfathers

Salomón Lovato

I remember that my two grandfathers lived with my mom, with us, because they were both widowers. The only thing is that my grandfather on my mother's side, was older than my paternal grandfather. But they were both quite old. My maternal grandfather died at the age of eighty-seven. My other grandfather passed away at eighty-one or something like that. Fact is, they both had a lot of experience.

But there they were, the two little old men. There was nothing to do. My grandfather, on my father's side, was very shrewd. He owned sheep; he had money. When he became a widower women took everything away from him. And my other grandfather, that was a different story; he was poor to begin with. He was a farmer; that's all. He liked to whittle with his pocket knife. But he was a poet. He composed lots of verses. He was a very wise, very intelligent man, but he didn't have an education. In any case, he was very much a chicken. Not my paternal grandfather, he wasn't, ah, he wasn't afraid of anything. He wasn't. He was even kind of a cut-up.

Very well. Both of them used to get together to chat about old times. "You compadre," one of them would say, "you didn't even go to the States. I did. I got to fight the Indians and you didn't. You're here, you were born here, and you're going to die here," he'd tell him. The other one would retort: "If I die before you compadre," my pop Ignacio, the shrewd one, would say to my pappy Telesfor. I'd call one of them pop and the other pappy. "If I die before you I'm going to come and pull you by your legs."

My pappy Telesfor lived, oh, a little ways from our house. I'll be darned if pop Ignacio didn't die first, the one who told my pappy that he'd return to pull his legs, so that my pappy Telesfor no longer wanted to live alone.

Un pobrecito indio

Salomón Lovato

Estaba un cuento que contaba mi agüelito. Éste era un indio que andaba, muy pobrecito, y andaba aá en mi tierra. Y estaba una gente muy rica. Y el pobrecito indio ya se andaba muriendo de hambre. En la andada que andaba él se jalló una piedra y se jue y entró a pedir agua. Tenían un banquete, esta gente rica. Eso me contaba mi agüelo a mí. Banquete grande. Y el pobre indio estaba allí muriéndose de hambre. Y loo sacó la piedra, y es que le dice: "¿Cuánto vale esta piedra hermano?" es que le dice al del banquete.

Pus era oro, ¿sabes? Pus de una vez le pusieron la mesa. Tráiganle a este pobre hombre comida, y pacá y pallá, y de una vez le llenaron el plato. Y loo le dice, cuando ya acabó de comer el indio, le dice el del banquete:

—¿Ónde jallates esta piedra?

—Pus yo no sé hermano—le dice—. Yo no sé si en esta loma, o esta loma, o otra loma, pero yo ya estoy lleno. Munchas gracias—les dice.

A Poor Little Old Indian

Salomón Lovato

There's a story my grandfather used to tell. It was about this Indian who was very, very poor, who roamed all over in my neck of the woods. And there were these very rich folks. The poor little old Indian was practically starving to death. In one of his outings he found a rock so he went and knocked at the door to ask for a drink of water. These rich folks were having a banquet. That's what my grandfather used to tell me. A huge banquet. And the poor Indian was starving to death. Then he took out his stone and is to have said to the man in charge of the banquet: "How much is this stone worth, my brother?"

You see, it was gold. Right away they set up the table for him. Bring this poor man something to eat and this or that. Right away they filled up his plate. And then when the Indian finished eating, the man in charge of the banquet said to him:

"Where did you find this stone?"

"Well I don't know brother," he said to him. "I don't know if it was on this hill, or this one, or some other hill, but, at any rate, I'm full. Thanks very much!"

Por un voto perdí

Adrián Chávez

Yo le voy a platicar una cosita, ya que estamos hablando de la
política, algo que yo vide antes de ser votante. Yo siempre andaba, quizás, viendo lo que no me importaba—y oyendo. Pues
no quiero alargala muncho, pero del Condao de Sandoval de Bernalillo eran los caudillos. Éstos iban aá al Río Puerco. Pos en una
ocasión, estos compadres aá en Gualupe, uno de ellos iba correr
pa juez de paz o no sé qué.

—¿Qué le parece compadre?

—Pos me dicen que me dan esta chanza.

—Como usted quiera compadre.

—¿Me va a ayudar compadre?

—Yo creo que sí—le dijo—, pero pos yo no sé nada de esas
cosas compadre. No sé nada.

—Güeno. ¿Me ayuda?

Quedaron en eso. Cuando se llegó la elección, jueron a
Gualupe de Bernalillo los Montoya; eran los meros, meros. Estaban esperando que llegara la gente a votar. Y en eso llegó el
compadre, no el que iba a correr pa juez de paz o lo que juera.

—Oiga. ¿Qué nos va a ayudar?

—¿Por quién?

—Por esto.

—No. Ya quedé con mi compadre, oiga.

—Pero mire—le dijo uno de ellos.

Dejaron cae un veinte, ¿ves?

—Que no, que . . .

Dejaron cae otro. Y así se lo jueron llevando. Y le platicaban.

—Mire, que va a estar mejor la harina . . .

Y el compadre nomás se torcía. Cuando ya estaba güena,
quizás, la pilita, le dio el compadre en la torre.

Güeno. Era poca la gente; en el día votaban todos ai. Muy
temprano ya contaban los votos. En la misma noche casi se supo

quiénes habían ganao, y el compadre éste no jallaba cómo hacer con su compadre con el que había quedao mal. En la mañana se topó con él.

—Güenos días compadre.

—Güenos días. ¿Cómo le jue?

—Mal compadre. Nomás por un votó perdí—le dijo.

Le quiso decir que causa de él había perdido.

—Pues compadre, como le dije, yo no sé nada de esas cosas. Pero este muchacho—le dijo—, que muchacho tan brillante. Pus él me jue explicando palabra por palabra y apilonando los billetes.

—Güeno—le dijo—, tiene razón.

I Lost By One Vote

Adrián Chávez

Since we're talking about politics, I'm going to tell you a little something, something that I saw before I became a registered voter. I guess I was always watching and listening to things that weren't any of my business. Well, I don't want to stretch the point very much, but the political bosses were from Bernalillo, in Sandoval County. These fellows used to go over to the Río Puerco. Well, one time one of these compadres in Guadalupe decided to run for justice of the peace or what have you.

"What do you think compadre?"

"Well they tell me I've got a pretty good chance."

"Whatever you say compadre."

"Are you going to vote for me compadre?"

"I believe so," he said to him, "but I don't know anything about those things compadre. I don't know a thing."

"Nonetheless. Will you help me out?"

They agreed that he would. When the election rolled around, the Montoyas from Bernalillo went to Guadalupe. They were the real big shots. They were waiting for the people to arrive at the polls. About that time one of the compadres arrived, not the one who was a candidate for justice of the peace. Then two of the Montoya politicians approached him.

"Listen. Are you going to help us out?"

"Who for?"

"You know."

"No. Listen. I already agreed to help my compadre out."

"But look," said one of them to him.

You see, they dropped a twenty dollar bill in front of him.

"Why no, because . . ."

They dropped another twenty dollar bill. And that's the way they kept him going. And they kept on coaxing him.

"Listen, I assure you that the price of flour is going to be better . . ."

And the compadre all he could do was shrug his shoulders. I guess when the little pile of bills looked pretty good, the compadre got the better of the politicians.

Very well, the number of people on election day was small; everyone voted in one day. The votes were counted very early. On same night just about everyone knew who had been elected, and the compadre didn't know what to do about his other compadre whom he had crossed. On the following morning he ran into him.

"Good morning compadre."

"Good morning. How did you do?"

"Bad compadre. I lost by only one vote," he said to him.

He implied that he had lost because of him.

"Well compadre, as I told you, I don't know anything about these kinds of things. But this fellow," he said to him, "what an intelligent guy! Why he explained to me word for word all about politics while at the same time piling up the money bills."

"Very well," he said to him. "You're right."

El velorio

Salomón Lovato

Me acuerdo yo que no había cajonerías. No había nada, pero hacían cajones, hacían el cajón entre todos. Se juntaban. Lo hacían. Los hombres hacían el cajón y las mujeres ponían el velo, ponían todo. Iban y traiban velo, y traiban too, y lo ponían allí en una mesa de lada.

Pero te voy a platicar una historia. Yo estaba muy chiquito. Yo no me acuerdo quién sería que se murió pero toos velaban a esa persona, porque lo querían, y lo mostraban. En esta ocasión estaba yo muy chiquito y me quedé. Llamaron a toos a comer y yo me quedé onde estaba el muerto. Era un cuarto largo, dispensa le decían. Ai estaba el muerto. Y le ponían una sábana larga que se tapaba toa la mesa pa bajo. Me quedé yo allí solo; no había nadien con quien platicar quizás. Yo nomás jui de los chamacos, porque había pura gente grande. Me quedé yo sentao y cuando menos acordé comenzó: "Rrr-rre," y yo me quedé muy escuchadito. "¿Qué está pasando aquí?" Se me pusieron las greñas pa arriba. Y la gente estaba plática y plática aá en la cocina. Y loo jui y le dije, no me acuerdo si le dije a mi mamá, que alguna cosa estaba sonando.

—¡Oh!—me dijo—. ¿Qué va a estar?

—Sí—le dije.

Alguna cosa estaba sonando. Toca que se había metido un perro abajo y ai estaba dormido. Estaba roncando.

The Wake

Salomón Lovato

I recall there being no mortuaries. There were none, but caskets were made nonetheless. Everyone got together and pitched in. They got the job done. The men built the casket and the women put white gauze veil around it and everything else. They'd go and fetch the veil and everything else and put it on a table made of cistus (apparently flexible boughs that provided a soft resting place).

But I'm going to tell you a story. I was very small. I don't know who died, but everybody was keeping vigil over that person, because they loved him, and people showed their love. On this particular occasion I was very small and so I stayed back. Everybody was called to eat, but I stayed where the deceased person was. It was a long room; it was called a pantry. That's where the dead person was. It had a bed sheet that covered the entire table and draped all the way down. I stayed behind, alone; there was no one to talk to, I guess. Of the children I was the only one who went because there were only older people at the wake. I remained seated and when I least expected it, a noise started: "Rrr-rre," and I remained very quietly. "What's going on here?" My hair stood on end. And the people were yackety-yak in the kitchen. Then I went and said something to someone, I don't know if it was my mom, that something was making a noise.

"Oh!," she said to me. "It's nothing!"

"Yes there is," I said to her.

Something was making a noise. It so happens that a dog had gotten underneath the table (where the deceased person lay) and there it was asleep. It was snoring.

La plebe

Salomón Lovato

Los casorios eran una cosa muy bonita, pero antes de que yo llegué a ver casorios, ya que, güeno chiquito, toavía andaban con teguas. No traiban zapatos. ¡Teguas! Y bailaban en la tierra; no había salas. Bailaban en la tierra; unos polvaderones y traiban un hombre o una señora echando agua pa que se quitara el polvo. Muy chiquito lo vide. ¡Eso hace muncho tiempo! Muy poquito me tocó ver.

Y loo la plebe de Guadalupe—yo los quiero a todos—ai es onde no caiba bien el negocio, porque siempre entraban con las espuelas puestas al baile. ¡No todos! Pero algunos, había algunos. Y los de San Luis también. Y pa la gente grande, pa mí no, pero pa la gente grande, era un insulto que jueran entrando contoy espuelas o con el sombrero. Aá no podía bailar una persona con el sombrero. Te lo quitaban. Si era un baile privao, te quitabas el sombrero.

Me tocó ver este señor, no te voy a decir su nombre, pus el porecito andaba con el sombrero puesto, y no se lo quitaba. "¡Quítate el sombrero!" ¡No! Pus aá en medio de la sala se lo quitaron. Y no hizo nada el porecito. Estaba calvo. No tenía ni un cabello. Eso le dio vergüenza a él. Pero no, no pasó nada. Pero los viejos viejos, no les gustaba que la plebe bailara con sombrero.

Kids

Salomón Lovato

Weddings were a very beautiful thing, but before I was able to observe them, at a time when I was still very small, people still wore moccasins. People didn't wear shoes. Moccasins! And people danced on dirt floors; there weren't any dance halls. They danced on the dirt. What huge clouds of dust! People had a man or a woman who went around sprinkling water to cut down the dust. I was very small when I saw all of that. That was a long time ago! I got to see very little of that sort of thing, but see I did.

And then the young guys from Guadalupe—I love them all— that's where they pushed their luck, because they always entered the dance hall wearing their spurs. Not all of them! But some did; there were some who did. And those from San Luis did so too. For the older people, not for me, but for the older people, it was an insult for the young guys to go in the dance wearing their spurs and hat. A man wasn't allowed to dance with his hat on. They'd jerk it away from you. If it was a private dance, you took off your hat.

I got to see this man, I'm not going to tell you his name. Well, the poor thing was wearing his hat and he wouldn't take it off. "Take off your hat." No! Well in the middle of the dance hall they removed it. The poor thing didn't do anything. He was bald-headed. He didn't have a single hair. That embarrassed him. But no, nothing happened. But the old men, the very old, they didn't appreciate young guys dancing with their hats on.

Borracheras

Nasario P. Garcia

¡Yo me llegué a poner algunas borracheras, eh, de mulas! No te digo que una vez entré a caballo a la sala de don Porfirio en la placita de Gualupe. Antonces había entrao yo de vaquero con un hombre que iba a llevar vacas paá pal Alto. Al fin me enojé y me arrendé. Y tenían un bautismo ai en el Cabezón, y yo y mi compañero que andaba conmigo, medio nos embolamos, ai en el Cabezón. Pues ya veníanos embolaos. Tocó que jue en papá y él se trujo mi caballo que usaba yo con la cama y todo. Y ya nos vinimos noche, yo y mi compañero, y haciéndose oscuro, ya estaba el baile a case del dijunto Porfirio. Pues entré hasta dentro de la sala en el caballo. ¡Todo borracho! Me agarró. Me *agarró* y me apeó del caballo, nomás que el caballo era muy pataleón.

Pero ese caballo, era malo el caballo, y pataleón, pero ese caballo yo lo hacía entrar a una casa. Ondequiera que yo le daba entraba ese caballo. Y era malo el caballo.

Oh, en ese tiempo tendría yo como diez y ocho años, quizás, y no, pus salieron todas las mujeres a juir (risas).

Sprees

Nasario P. García

Why I, ah, really hung on some good drunks, with moonshine!
As I told you, once I went in on horseback to Don Porfirio's
dance hall located in Guadalupe's plaza. At that time I had just
decided to become a cowhand, joining a man who was going to
have a cattle drive to a place called El Alto (The High Spot). No
sooner I joined him, I got mad and turned back. There in
Cabezón a baptism was taking place, and I and my companion
who was with me sort of got drunk. There in Cabezón. Why we
were pretty loaded, in fact. It so happened that my dad went to
Cabezón and he brought back the horse that I was using for carrying my bedroll and everything. It was already quite late when
my friend and I left Cabezón. No sooner it got dark and the
dance at the late Don Porfirio's house was underway. Why I
went way in to the dance hall on my horse. Dead drunk! Don
Porfirio grabbed me. He *grabbed* me and brought me down off
the horse, the only thing being that the horse was quite a kicker.

Why that horse was mean, and, as I say, quite a kicker, but
that horse I could make him go in a house. Anywhere I directed
him, that horse would go in. The horse was really mean.

I would say that back in those days, ah, I must have been
about eighteen years old. Why all those ladies (in the dance hall)
took off-and-running (laughter).

Un tiroteo

Adelita Gonzales

Muncho licor tomaban pa días de fiesta en Gualupe. Munchas veces no había por qué se pelearan, pero se embolaban. Y tú sabes un embolao; es terco y al fin se pegaban unos a los otros.

Yo me acuerdo una vez que se pelearon—se me hace a mí que como que se encelaban los de un lugarcito a otro—los muchachos de Salazar. No querían que los muchachos de Gualupe platicaran con las de Salazar. Y los de Gualupe no querían que los de Salazar platicaran con las muchachas de Gualupe. De ai venían los pleitos. Y se pelearon esta vez, muncho, bastante, hasta tiroteo.

Y me acuerdo que estaba un hombre que ya tenía tirao a otro. Era de estos Romero; eran poco gallardos pa pelear. Y vino mi compadre Alberto y les tiró con una piedra y le pegó a uno de ellos. Y se cayó el hombre. Pues ai lo soltó. Una pelea grande.

Balazos y todo tiraban, pero no se mataban. ¡Gracias a Dios que ni se lastimaban!

A Shoot 'Em Up

Adelita Gonzales

A lot of liquor was consumed on holidays in Guadalupe. Often there was no rhyme or reason why men should get in a fight, but it usually came about as a result of getting drunk. And you know what a drunk person is like; he's stubborn. Finally they'd end up beating each other up.

I remember once that the boys from Salazar got into a fight. It seems to me that the boys from one little village became jealous of those from another village. They didn't want for the boys from Guadalupe to chat with the girls from Salazar. And those from Guadalupe didn't want for those from Salazar to talk with the girls from Guadalupe. That's how these disputes came about. And they got into it this one time, quite a bit, in fact. Shots were even fired.

And I recall that this man already had this other one down. He belonged to the Romeros from Salazar; they were pretty good fighters. And here comes my compadre Alberto (from Guadalupe) and threw a rock and struck one of them. And the man tumbled over. That's when he turned the man who was down loose. It was a big fight.

Bullets and everything were fired, but they never killed each other. Thank goodness they didn't even get hurt.

Chapter 4: Mischief

Dos padres

Adrián Chávez

Estaban estos dos padres, y uno de ellos era muy tomador. Tomaba muncho. A veces no sabía ni que andaba tomao, pero, de todos modos, siempre iba a ver a su compañero, muy seguido. En una de estas ocasiones dejó de tomar.

Pues una mañana salió a depositar un sobre y no sabía dónde estaba la estafeta. Aá más adelante se encontró un niño. Ya le habla el padre:

—Oye güen niño—le dice—. ¿Y dónde está la estafeta por aquí?

—Pos ai, tantas cuadras pallá.

—¿Y por qué no juites a la escuela hoy?

—No, pos por esta y esta razón.

Empezó aconsejalo el padre:

—Mira hijito—le dice—. Vale más que vayas a la escuela; es muy importante. ¿Eres cristiano?

—Sí y no.

—Vale más que le pongas más sentido—le dice—, porque pa que los güenos niños como tú conozcan el camino pal cielo, y esto y el otro.

—¡Um jum! Pero usted tanto que ha rezao—le dijo el niño—, y no sabe ni siquiera el camino pa la estafeta.

Two Priests

Adrián Chávez

Once there were these two priests, and one of them was quite a drinker. He loved liquor. At times he didn't even know he was drunk, but, at any rate, he always went to visit his pal, quite frequently, in fact. On one of his trips he gave up drinking.

Well, one morning he took off to mail a letter but didn't know where the post office was. On up ahead he ran into a little boy, so the priest talked to him:

"Listen my good child," he says to him. "Where's the post office around here?"

"Well, over there, a few blocks up ahead."

Out of the clear blue sky, the priest said to him:

"And why didn't you go to school today?"

"Well, you see, because of this and that."

The priest started to give him advice:

"Listen my dear son," he says to him. "You had better go to school; it's very important. Are you a Christian?"

"Yes and no."

"You better think more about that," he says to the child, "so that good children such as yourself are better acquainted with the road to heaven, and so on and so forth."

"Well said! But for someone like you who has prayed so much," said the child to the priest, "how come you don't even know the way to the post office?"

Una vaca muy brava

Salomón Lovato

Te voy a platicar un secreto. Ai en el Cabezón tenía don Rosendo García, ése era el que tenía poquitas más vacas. Güeno, y mi suegro don Rudolfo, pero este hombre tenía su corral allí en el Cabezón, y le dijieron dos hombres del gobierno: "Encierra las vacas."

Venían dos hombres del gobierno. Entraron. Tenía don Rosendo García corral de latas, de esas latas que están paradas. La puerta era de madera, y estábanos asina, tanto asina como un pie, un pie y medio de este modo. Pus encerraron las vacas los del gobierno, y este hombre, don Rosendo, tenía una vaca muy brava. No podía entrar naiden en el corral y la encerró con según intención pa que no le cortaran munchas vacas, tú sabes. Pus encerró las vacas y nosotros estábanos todos en redondo del corral a ver a quién le iba, a quién le iba a tocar que le pegara. ¡Y tenía los cuernos puntiagudos!

Y el cuento es que se metieron estos hombres y las vacas más bonitas, y las más gordas eran las que marcaban con una . . . tenían que matalas. Y entraron estos hombres y les dijo él, don Rosendo García, que estaba esa vaca brava.

—¡Oh!—le dijo uno de ellos—, no son las primeras que hemos marcao.

La vaca estaba aá en un rincón echándose que parecía que le salía lumbre por los ojos porque era muy mal animal. Pues nada, comenzaron. Nomás en cuanto comenzaron cuando se vino la vaca. Y estaba un hombre que pesaba como doscientas libras; el otro no, estaba poco delgadito. Y se vino la vaca. ¡Y sabes tú que ese hombre pesao pasó por entre medio de las tablas! Quebró una de las tablas. Nomás en cuanto no lo agarró. Y se salvó don Rosendo García de vacas, de que le mataran vacas. Sí le mataron algunas pero no le volvieron a entrar más el corral. Ése jue uno de los incidentes.

Mi agüelo y en papá tenían pilas de borregas onde se las mataba el gobierno. ¡Pilas! Quiero decir, teníanos que trae leña y quemalas. ¿Sabes que a la gente que no tenía animales, se los daban? Pero ya no quería la gente; ya tenían más carne que ya no podían. Tenían carne seca hasta pa tirar pa arriba.

A Very Mean Cow

Salomón Lovato

I'm going to tell you a secret. There in Cabezón don Rosendo
García, he's the one who had a few more cattle than the others.
Okay, and so did my father-in-law, Don Rudolfo, but this man
had his corral in Cabezón, and two government officials said to
him: "Lock up your cows."

Two government officials showed up. They went in the corral.
Don Rosendo García had a corral made of narrow thin posts that
stood up (not buried), tied together with wire. The gate was
made of lumber, and there we were about a foot, a foot and a
half from the gate. Well, the government officials had the cows
locked up and this man, Don Rosendo García, had a very mean
cow. Usually no one could enter the corral because of it and so
he locked it up with certain ulterior motives; that is, so they
wouldn't cut too many of his cattle. Well, he locked up his cows
and the rest of us were all around the corral watching to see
whom the cow would go after, to see whom it was going to
strike. It had very sharp horns!

The fact is that these government officials got into the corral
and the most beautiful and fattest cows were the ones they
marked with a . . . they had to slaughter them. (The number ex-
ceeded that allowed by the government.) These men went in
and Don Rosendo García warned them that that was a mean
cow.

"No sweat," responded one of them, "it's not the first time
we've come across one like it."

The cow was in a corner gearing itself up as though fire were
coming out its eyes because it was a mean animal. So much for
that. The men started selecting the cows to be slaughtered. No
sooner they started when the cow went after them. One of the
men weighed about two hundred pounds; the other one was a
bit skinnier. And here comes the cow. And wouldn't you know

it, the fat man found himself going through two peeled poles that the corral was made of? He broke one of them. The cow barely missed him. As a result Don Rosendo García was able to save some of his cows; he kept some of them from getting killed. They did kill some but the officials never again entered his corral. That's one of the incidents that comes to mind.

My grandfather and my dad had gobs of sheep which the government ordered killed. A bunch! I mean, we had to gather firewood and burn them. Do you know that the officials gave the dead stock to those people who didn't have any! But people didn't want any more meat; they had more than they could handle. They had jerky coming out of their ears.

La corrida del gallo

Adelita Gonzales

Pal tiempo como ora el día de San Juan, corrían a caballo. Les daban un gallo; y este gallo lo enterraban vivo. Se juntaban de veinte de a caballo, treinta de a caballo. Se iban alistando. Aá estaba el pobre gallo vivo y enterrao. Pasaban galopeando ellos a ver quién agarraba el gallo. Se paraban en línea y pasaban a ver qué agarraban. ¡Nada! ¡Nada! No lo agarraba naide. Al fin había uno.

Ellos iban vestidos de blanco; con la camisa blanca. Luego que sacaban el gallo, partía el que sacaba el gallo y les daba con el gallo. Uno contra los otros. Él mesmo pa que no se lo quitaran, él mesmo iba dándoles asina (de las patas) con el gallo. Él iba adelante y si se arrimaba uno le pegaba en tal de que no se le quitara su gallo. Quedaban las camisas blancas llenas de sangre. Como hasta que llegaba a la línea. Y el que llevaba el gallo, ése ganaba, ése agarraba el premio. A munchos les daban diez pesos; a munchos les daban un cajón de cerveza pa que se jueran todos a beber. Munchos, licor le daban al que sacaba el gallo.

Munchas veces hasta mi agüelito les dio el gallo pa la corrida. Iban a pedir, que no jallaban. "Yo les daré gallo," les decía. Mi agüelito y mi mamá Juanita les daban gallo pa que jueran a enterrar aá.

Pues había veces que cuanto más un gallo le podían admitir. ¡Oh! Trabajaban muncho porque lo enterraban bastante hondo. De aquí que sacaran aquel gallo, porque tenían que ir corriendo hasta que sacaba el gallo alguno.

Una vez, no se lastimó naiden, pero se cayó uno de los caballos y ai se jueron volcando todos. ¡Oh! Estaba miedo cuando corrían esos caballos asina. Caiban unos arriba de otros. Pero el que sacaba el gallo, ése se iba con él pa que no se lo quitaran.

The Rooster Race

Adelita Gonzales

At times like now for Saint John's day, they'd run on horseback. The men were given a rooster; and this rooster was buried alive with its neck sticking out. Twenty or thirty on horseback would gather around. They'd start getting ready. There was that poor rooster, alive and buried up to its neck. The men on horseback (the *galleros*) galloped past the rooster to see who would grab it. They stood in line and then took off galloping to try their luck at plucking the bird. Nothing! Nothing! No one was able to grab it. Finally someone did.

The galleros were dressed in white; that is, a white shirt. Once the rooster was plucked out, the lucky one would take off striking the others with it trying to fend them off. One against the others, so they wouldn't wrest it from him. Until he crossed the finish line, he'd strike them with the rooster by holding it by the legs. The gallero with the rooster would lead the pack so as to avoid having the rooster taken away. The white shirts were left soaked in blood. Whoever got to the finish line with the rooster won; he received an award. Many got ten dollars; others received a case of beer so everyone could go off and celebrate. Still other villagers donated liquor to the lucky gallero.

Often times even my own grandfather donated the rooster for the race. The participants would go and ask for one because they couldn't find one. "I'll give you one," he'd tell them. My grandfather and my mother Juanita used to give away the rooster for the contest.

Why there were times when only one rooster would suffice. Oh! The galleros struggled a lot because they'd bury it quite deeply. By the time they plucked it out, it took a long time, because they had to keep trying until someone turned the trick. One time, no one was hurt, but one of the horses fell, and from then on all the others tumbled over. Oh, it was scary whenever the horses ran like that. One horse tumbled over the others. But the one who plucked out the rooster, he took off so no one would take it away from him until he crossed the finish line.

Dos jóvenes astrónomos

Eduardo Valdez

Éste es un caso que pasó con dos jóvenes que estudiaban y querían ser astrónomos. Un día salieron de la suidá al campo. Querían ver los astros del cielo y estudiar las estrellas y llegaron en casa de una viejita que vivía sola en un rancho. Esta viejita era muy pobrecita. No tenía más que un cuartito, y adelante del cuartito un cerquito donde tenía un burrito. Este burrito, cuando iba a llover, retozaba y se ponía muy contento, y la viejita ya sabía que iba a llover.

Los jóvenes le pidieron pasada y la viejita les dice:

—Jóvenes. No tengo más que este cuartito y nomás una cama.

Y les *dijo* que esa noche iba a llover. No importó. Los jóvenes le dijieron que ellos dormían allí afuera, que traiban sus camas y comida, y que ellos querían estudiar los astros del cielo porque estudiaban para astrónomos. La viejita les dice:

—Bien, cuando llegue la lluvia, entren aquí adentro para que no se mojen.

Los jóvenes se decían uno al otro: "¿Cómo sabe esta mujer que va a llover?"

—Pregúntale tú que te diga cómo sabe que va a llover cuando no hay ni nubes—dijo uno de ellos.

Antonces el otro de los jóvenes le preguntó:

—Señora, ¿cómo sabe usted que esta noche va a llover?

La viejita les dijo:

—¿Ven ese burrito en el cerquito? Cuando él retoza y está alegre, por cierto viene lluvia. No hay engaño.

A poco que oscureció, se comenzaron a poner nubes. En poco rato comenzó la lluvia y los jóvenes metieron sus camas al cuar-

tito; llovió toda la noche. Por la mañana uno de los jóvenes
mueve a su compañero y le dice:

—¡Levántate! Vamos antes que amanezca. Es una vergüenza
que un burro sepa más que nosotros.

Y se fueron y la viejita se quedó dormida.

Chapter 4: Mischief

Two Aspiring Young Astronomers

Eduardo Valdez

This is an incident involving two young men who were studying to become astronomers. One day they left the city to go out into the countryside. They wanted to observe the heavenly bodies and study the stars, and so they came upon this little old lady who lived alone on a ranch. This little old lady was very poor. All she had was a small room, and in front of it she had a small fence where she kept a donkey. This donkey, whenever it was going to rain, would frolic about and get very happy. The little old lady herself already knew that it was going to rain.

The young men asked her for lodging and the little old lady says to them:

"Young men. The only thing I have is this small room and just one bed."

She *told* them that it was going to rain that night. Just the same, the young men told her that they had their own bedding and food and that they would sleep outside because they wanted to study the heavenly bodies since they were studying to become astronomers. The little old lady says to them:

"Very well. When the rain comes, come inside so you won't get wet."

The young men said to each other:

"How does this lady know that it's going to rain?"

"You ask her to tell you how she knows that it's going to rain when there aren't even any clouds," said one of them.

Then the other young man asked her:

"Ma'am, how do you know that it's going to rain tonight?"

The little old lady responded:

"Do you see that donkey that's in the little fence? Whenever he's happy and frisks and jumps about, for sure the rain's coming. There's no ifs, ands, or buts about it."

Shortly after it got dark, clouds began to appear. A short while later it started to rain, and the young men brought their bedding into the small room; it rained all night long. In the morning one of them shakes his pal and says to him:

"Get up! Let's go before it's daybreak. It's a disgrace that a jackass knows more than us."

And so they took off, and the little old lady stayed in bed sleeping.

5

The Supernatural

Since people in rural areas spent a lot of time alone, some of it at night, hearing strange noises and even seeing peculiar things, whether through hallucination or some other unexplainable reason, was not uncommon. The reasons for these occurrences ranged from fear to superstition. It is worthwhile noting that most of the stories in this chapter take place at night; few accounts related to the supernatural, witchcraft, sorcery and the like ever occurred during the day. At the same time, one must not leave the impression that every individual in a community believed or accepted stories passed from one person or generation to another. Skepticism was not unusual, especially among those who viewed the stories as far-fetched at best, and improbable at worst. Even some individuals who were very religious tended to believe that they were not immune from the supernatural.

Many residents of the Río Puerco Valley believed in different types of supernatural events. Some of them, such as Bencés Gabaldón in "A Ball of Fire," could relate personal experiences and incidents which had been told to them by friends in a most convincing manner. Of course, some people, as mentioned above, did not believe in such stories, and others were not quite sure.

As a child, I often heard stories about enchanted places (*lugares encantados*), and at least one of these places seemed to have existed in every community. For example, Guadalupe had El Coruco (The Bedbug)—mentioned in "Chains Rattled"—that was known for its strange noises at night. San Luis was renowned for its Mesa where moving lights frequently appeared at night. Ghostly apparitions, such as those related in "The Man Who Hitched a Ride" and "The Doll," were not uncommonly reported.

Natural phenomena undoubtedly are the basis for some of the tales of witchcraft, as in the stories: "Seeing Things," "A Ball of Fire," and "An Indian."

In the Hispano communities along the Río Puerco, it was a practice for a family to name one of their sons Juan. If they had no sons, a daughter would be named Juana, for the name brought with it magical powers, including the ability to recognize and control witches, and the power to lift the spell of an evil eye (*mal ojo*). In "Two Witches and Two Fellows Named Juan," my great grandfather, who was blind, supposedly had the power to sense from a distance the presence of witches, to capture them, and to impose a price for giving them their freedom.

Stories of Navajo witchcraft were also told to me by some of the people with whom I talked. This is not too surprising, considering the many years that the Indians and Hispanos of the Río Puerco Valley were neighbors.

The *sujarana* spoken of in "Witchcraft" was a person of some importance in at least one Hispanic community—San Luis. It was she to whom a person went when someone had been the victim of sorcery for she had the power to discover who had cast the spell.

Cosas de esas

Luciano Sánchez

En papá y munchas otras gentes de Gualupe platicaban que volaban las brasas así como un trenecito. Pero yo nunca llegué a ver brasas. En ese tiempo no había nada cosas de esas. Lo que llegué a jallar en casa, en ese tiempo, antes de venirnos pa Alburquerque, llegamos a jallar güevos ai adelante de la casa. Sí teníanos gallinas y todo, pero todas estaban en el gallinero.

Y llegamos a jallar manzanas muy relumbrosas, bien, bien vidriosas, tamién sin haber manzanas allá ni nada. Taavía cuando va un frutero o alguien pues antonces puede uno decir, puede uno creer que sí. Pues no. Llegamos a echar en la estufa todo eso. Nosotros nunca llegamos agarrar nada, pa comer, diremos. Teníanos miedo. Porque de ver aquella manzana ai, sin saber diónde vino. ¡Mal!

Strange Things

Luciano Sánchez

My dad and many other people from Guadalupe would talk about flying sparks in the shape of a small train. But I never got to see flying sparks. Back then those strange things didn't exist. What I did discover at home, back then, before coming to Albuquerque, we did discover eggs right in front of our house. Yes, we had chickens, but they were all in the chicken coop. We also got to find very shiny apples, very, very glass-like, and that's without their being any apples or any other fruit around. At least when a fruit vendor or someone like that goes then one can believe or accept things like that. But no. We always burned all of that stuff in the stove. We never kept anything, that is to say, to eat. We were afraid. Just to look at that apple, without knowing where it came from, was bad business.

Sonaron cadenas

Adelita Gonzales

Munchos creiban verdaderamente en brujerías que venían más antes. Creiban en eso. Yo nunca creí en nada de eso; ni creibo. ¡Quién sabe! Puede que sí haiga.

Hubo una vez mi esposo, yo no sé cómo. Iba Salvador, iba y cuando pasó en frente de El Coruco sonaron cadenas. ¡Qué aquel hombre llegó a en casa casi como desmayao! ¡No sé cómo! Y loo le dije:

—¿Qué, qué pasa?

Llegó y nos gritó:

—Vengan. Vamos conmigo a desensillar el caballo.

Ya era en la noche. Venía de a case de don Teodoro García. Y logo le dije yo:

—¿Qué, qué pasó?

—Yo no sé—dijo—. Vamos conmigo. Desensillen el caballo y cierren la puerta—les dijo a las muchachas.

Dice él que cuando pasó que sonaron cadenas ai en El Coruco y el caballo se espantó. Y le digo:

—Yo no sé.

Puede que sí pasen esas cosas. Yo nunca tuve sustos asina.

Tú sabes doña Melesia y todos ellos, puede que ella te haiga platicao; a ella sí que se le apareció un burrito.

Yo no, oye. Yo nunca, nunca en mi vida que tengo no vide tal cosa así.

Chains Rattled

Adelita Gonzales

Many persons really believed in witchcraft of yesteryear. They believed in that sort of thing. I never did, and still don't. Who knows! Perhaps there is such a thing.

Once something happened to my husband; I don't know how. Salvador was on his way home and when he went by a place called El Coruco (The Bedbug) chains rattled. So much so that that poor man got home as though he was fainted! I don't know how it came about! Then I said to him:

"What, what's wrong?"

As he arrived he shouted at us:

"Come. Come with me to unsaddle the horse."

It was already night. He was on his way back from don Teodoro García's house. Then I said to him:

"What, what happened?"

"I don't know," he responded. "All of you come with me. Unsaddle the horse and close the gate," he ordered the girls.

He claims that when he went by El Coruco chains rattled and the horse got startled. And I said to him:

"I don't know about that."

Perhaps those things do go on. I was never frightened like that.

You know Doña Melesia and all of them, perhaps she's told you, she did see a donkey. (A donkey appeared before her eyes.)

Not me. I never, never in my life ever saw such things as ghosts.

Un bulto

Nasario P. García

Una vez en San Luis, pus, eh, yo iba ya tarde, como a las tres de la mañana; iba a pie, cuando estábanos trabajando ai en el WPA. Esa noche había una de estas juntas de políticos y se jueron todos y de ai me jui yo a pie. Cuando yo ya llegué, que pasé la plaza de San Luis, eh, vide venir un bulto negro. Aquí viene todo el camino. Antonces yo dije: "Quizás viene alguien." Antes de llegar, como de aquí allá a la puerta, a unos cuatro, cinco pies, empecé a hablale, pero este, este bulto no contestaba nada. Era un bulto todo negro y cruzó el camino y entró asina a un chamisal. Después que ya se dirigió asina a la izquierda al chamisal, pal rumbo de la mesa, pues antonces me dio miedo a mí. Luego se apartó pallá el bulto ese, pal rumbo de la mesa, y yo me jui todo el camino pal campo. Yo le hablé pero sabrá Dios quién, quién, sería. Y todo lo que vide jue nomás un bulto negro de arriba hasta bajo, que me acuerdo yo. ¡Ya eran las tres de la mañana!

A Dark Object

Nasario P. García

One time in San Luis, well, ah, it was already late, like three o'clock in the morning, and I was on my way home. I was on foot. That's when we were working for the WPA. There had been one of those political meetings that night and everyone left, including myself. On foot. By the time I arrived, as I passed the village of San Luis, ah, I saw a dark object coming toward me. Here it comes right down the road. Then I said to myself: "I guess someone's coming." Before it got to where I was, like from here to the door, about four or five feet, I started to talk to it, but this object wouldn't answer. It was a black object all over; it crossed the road and went right into the sagebrush. After going left toward the sagebrush, by way of the mesa, then I got scared. Then that dark object took off that way, in the direction of the mesa, and I took off down the road for the campsite. I spoke to it but God knows who, who it was. And the only thing I saw was a dark object, from head to toe, as far as I can recollect. It was already three o'clock in the morning!

Chapter 5: The Supernatural

Visiones

Adrián Chávez

Yo conocí este señor. Ese hombre lo podía uno ver hacer visiones. Por ejemplo, iba en su caballo él, montao, y le llegó a causar visiones a otro compañero que iba con él. Por ejemplo, tiraba su cuarta y le dijía:

—Ya se me cayó mi cuarta. ¡Dámela!

Y se apeaba su compañero y cuando se iba a agachar, bien vido que lo iba a picar una víbora; se hacía víbora su cuarta de él. Al fin no la quiso agarrar. Tuvo que apearse Eduardo, el de las visiones, por la cuarta, y enseñale que no era víbora, que era su cuarta. Esto lo oí platicar yo. Eran vaqueros ellos los dos.

En otra vez cuando llegaron al rancho, entró el compañero de Eduardo pa dentro, y vido que se le vino encima una osa, de allí dionde estaba, onde dormía él en la camalta. Pues se le prendió él al osa de las orejas y andaba luchando con ella cuando ábrese Eduardo la puerta.

—¿Pero qué andas haciendo?—es que le dijo.

—Este animal . . .

Es que traiba una almuada.

—En una de éstas que me hagas reír, que te burles de mí, te voy a dar un balazo.

Pues se llevaban muy duro ellos los dos. Otra vez lo hizo Eduardo que se juera llenando el cuarto de agua. Se subió su compañero en una silleta, y cuando ya iba a subir más se dejó ir y cayó en el suelo . . . no en la agua.

Pues munchas de esas tonteras pasaban. Cómo las haría, ¡yo no sé! Ese hombre, Eduardo que le digo, me platicaba él que de joven anduvo muncho con los circos; ai aprendió él munchas cosas.

·

Seeing Things

Adrián Chávez

I knew this gentleman. One could see that man make things turn into something else. For example, he would be riding along on his horse and he'd manage to play tricks on a pal of his who was with him. He'd let drop his quirt and say to him:

"I dropped my quirt. Give it to me!"

His friend would get down from his horse and about the time he was going to stoop down to get it, he saw clearly that a snake was about to strike him. The quirt could turn into a snake. In the end he refused to grab it. Eduardo, the one who had the power to make people see things, had to get down off his horse to pick up his quirt and show his riding pal that it was not a snake. I heard people talk about all of this. The two of them were cowboys.

On another occasion when they got to the ranch, Eduardo's pal went inside the house where he slept, whereupon a female bear leaped at him. Well, he grabbed hold of the bear by the ears and here he was wrestling with it, when all of a sudden Eduardo opened the door.

"But what are you doing?," he said to him.

"This animal . . ."

He supposedly had ahold of a pillow.

"One of these days when you play a trick on me, and make fun of me, I'm going to put a bullet in you."

The two of them were very rough on each other. One other time Eduardo made him start filling up this room with water. His pal climbed on top of a chair, and, when the water was about to rise above him, he jumped and fell smack on the floor—not in the water.

As you can imagine, many of those silly things took place.

Chapter 5: The Supernatural

How Eduardo managed to do them, I don't have any idea! He used to tell me that as a young man he traveled quite a bit with the circus. That's where he learned a lot of those things.

El hombre que pidió pasaje

Damiano Romero

En una vez venía pacá pa Alburquerque, y aá cerca de San Luis, venía como las once del día. No venía tomao ni nada. Y ai en San Luis estaba un hombre y me pidió pasaje. Lo subí en la troca y caminé como unas cien yardas y loo le pregunté que si pa ónde iba y no me respondió. Lo vide yo que iba juntra mí. No me respondió. Poquito más aá le dije:

—¿Ónde quiere llegar? ¿A qué casa en San Luis?—porque ya estaba San Luis.

No me respondió. Nomás me vía, era todo. Cuando enfrenté la iglesia, lo de atrás de la iglesia, y el oratorio, volteé a hablale y ya no iba conmigo. Se apeó pero no sé ónde se apearía. Sin haber parao la troca; sin abrir la puerta. Ya no iba conmigo. ¡No sé qué sería! Un espíritu o qué sería. Y hay munchos que les he platicao pero no me creyen.

Munchas cosas llegaron a pasar a gente aá; como eran solos pues no les creiban. O ya si eran medio borrachos, "el señor, pues no, andaba borracho cuando las vido y too." Pero no, pasaban algunas cosas poco extrañas que no puede uno probar pero pasaban. Pasaban las cosas.

The Man Who Hitched a Ride

Damiano Romero

Once I was coming to Albuquerque, about eleven o'clock in the morning, and I wasn't drunk or anything. And there close to San Luis there was a man who asked me for a ride. I picked him up in my truck and drove him about one hundred yards and then asked him where he was headed and he didn't answer me. I saw him sitting right next to me. He didn't answer me. A little ways farther on I said to him:

"Where do you want me to drop you off? Which home in San Luis?," because we were almost in San Luis.

He didn't answer me. He only looked at me. That's all. When I came to the church, the back of the church, and the oratory, because the road is behind them, I turned around to talk to him, but he was no longer riding with me. He got off, but I don't know where. Without having stopped the truck; without having opened the door. He was no longer with me. I don't know what it was! A spirit or what have you. And I've talked to many individuals about this, but they don't believe me.

Many things happened at one time or another to people over in the Río Puerco, but, since they were alone, nobody ever believed them. Or if some individual liked liquor a little, they'd say that "why he was drunk when he saw those things and all," but no, things that were a bit strange, which can't be proven, used to occur. Those things just happened.

Chapter 5: The Supernatural

Luces

Damiano Romero

Había lugares que se vían luces y todo, sí. Nunca había nada pero se vían luces en ciertos lugares. Toavía ora mismo hay lugares en algunas casas viejas que están abandonadas, que mira uno de aá lejos, y viene uno una noche y se para y mira y hay luz en aquella casa y no hay naide ai. Ya está abandonao el lugar.

Yo mismo he visto luces en las casas. Por supuesto que cuando llega uno cerquita se apagan, pero nomás se retira uno y se güelven a prender. ¡No sé qué será! Dicen que hay tesoros, que hay algo aí. ¡Puede que haiga!

Pero ha tocao en otras ocasiones que he ido ya en la tarde, pa la luz de la tarde, he ido yo, mi muchacho y mi otro muchacho. Llegamos a ver carros, güeno, luces de carro arriba de las mesas de San Luis. Ai no hay camino ni nada. Y cuando llegó a la orilla de la mesa, se clavaban las luces abajo derecho sin haber camino. ¡No sé qué sería! Eso sí, iban dos muchachos conmigo. Cuando platico eso me creyen pocos, pero los demás no me creyen.

Lights

Damiano Romero

Yes, there were places where you could see lights and all of that stuff. One could never find anything, but lights were seen in certain places. Even now there's places, locations, in some old, abandoned homes, which can be seen from a distance, and you can pick a night and stand outside and take a look and there's a light in that certain house. And no one's living in it! The place is already abandoned.

I've seen lights myself in those homes. Of course when one gets close to them, they go out, but as soon as you walk away, they light up again. I don't know what it is! People say that there's hidden treasures or something. Perhaps that's true!

But on other occasions I've had the opportunity of having gone in the evening, at dusk, with my two boys. We got to see cars, I mean, car lights on top of the mesa at San Luis. There's no road there or anything, but when they reached the edge of the mesa, the lights pointed downward without there being a road. I don't know what it was! One thing for sure, my two boys were with me. Whenever I talk about this, a few people believe me, but the rest of them don't.

Chapter 5: The Supernatural

Un brasero

Bencés Gabaldón

Pues yo llegué a ver brujos, oiga. Una vez, en un tiempo, una gente que vivía ai cerquita de nosotros en San Luis se cambiaron a un lugar que iban a sembrar; enteramente iban ellos a sembrar. Se cambiaron de ai pa arriba, quizá como una milla o unas dos millas por ai. Se llevaron todo el garrero. Güeno, no quedó naiden en la casa; estaba vacía la casa. La casa que dejaron estaba cerquita. Puede que como unas, cuanto más, puede que hubiera cien yardas, de la casa de nosotros.

Pues de ai en la noche, en la tarde, ya oscuro, vino el muchacho que había llevao el garrero; vino a trae el carro de caballos pa case un tío mío. Pues que cuando iba pasando por su casa, que había quedao vacía, va saliendo un brasero bárbaro de ai y se le metió a las mulas aquí abajo, y arrancaron a juir con él, pa abajo, y aquel brasero metiéndosele a las mulas aquí en las patas. Se alumbraba bien alumbrao. Bien corría la lumbre, que parecía que tenían alumbrao con lámparas.

Y luego, luego juimos nosotros de ai de en casa, porque estaba cerquita, como dije. No había ni cien yardas. Juimos a ver, ¡y nada! No había nada. No se movía una paja. ¡Por nada! Y luego cuando nos vinimos ya estaba alumbrao otra vez. No había naiden. Estaba nomás la pura casa vacía. Sola. Salía el brasero por la chiminea, y cuando juimos nosotros no había naiden. ¡Yo lo vide! ¡Yo lo vide! ¡Y no es mentira!

Brasas que volaban

Bencés Gabaldón

¡Y luego verás te tú! Te voy a platicar otra cosa que vide yo tamién. Me acuerdo yo de un muchacho que se llamaba Juan
Mora. Este muchacho iba con flete de aquí de La Plaza pallá pa
San Luis. Cuando iba aá llegando al Río Puerco, se le prendió un
brasero a él, que no sabía qué era. Pues nomás no supo. No supo.
Yo no sé diónde demonio habría tantas brasas en esos tiempos,
oye. Yo me acuerdo que se podían parar arriba en los álamos; se
alumbraban los álamos. Yo lo llegué a ver yo. Eso sí lo llegué a ver
yo. Y no es mentira. No es mentira porque yo lo vide. Munchas
cosas pasaban asina. Munchas cosas. Sí. Eran brasas que volaban lo
mesmo que los oroplanos ora. Volaban por el viento.

A Ball Of Fire

Bencés Gabaldón

Well, I tell you, I got to see sorcerers. Once upon a time, a long time ago, a family who lived very close to us in San Luis moved to a place that they were going to sow. That's all they were going to do, sow it. They moved from San Luis northward, about a mile or two. Thereabouts. They took all of their junk. No one stayed back; the house was left empty. As I say, the house that these people left behind was very close to us. It must have been about, at the very most, about one hundred yards from our house.

Well from then on into the night, in the evening really, when it was already dark, the boy who had taken all of the family's junk returned. He came back to return the horse wagon to an uncle of mine. Well, about the time he was passing by his house, which had been left vacant, a terrible ball of fire started coming out from the house and got underneath the mules. They took off running with him, headed down range, and that ball of fire persisted in getting entangled in the mules' legs. The place was really lit up. The fire really traveled fast, to the point where it seemed like everything was illuminated with lanterns.

And then, then we went from our house because, as I said, it was close by. It wasn't one hundred yards away. We went to see. Nothing! There was nothing. Not even a straw could be seen moving. No matter how hard one tried! And then when we left, the house was lit up again. But there was no one home. The empty house was the only thing there. The house was alone. The sparks of fire could be seen coming out through the chimney, but when we went there, there wasn't anybody. I saw everything! I saw it! And that's no lie!

Sparks That Flew

Bencés Gabaldón

And something else too! I'm going to tell you something else I saw. I recall a young man named Juan Mora. This fellow was on his way with a wagon full of cargo from here in Albuquerque headed for San Luis. When he was about to approach the Río Puerco a huge ball of fire got ahold of him. He didn't know what it was. He simply didn't know. He didn't. I don't know where in the devil all of those sparks came from, back in those days. I remember that they could land on top of the trees and the trees lit up. I myself got to see it all. That I can attest to. And that's no lie. It's not a lie because I saw it. Many things like that would happen. Many. Yes. They were red sparks that flew the same way airplanes do so today. They flew through the sky.

Cosas extrañas

Benjamín "Benny" Lucero

¡Y cosas extrañas ha visto! Originalmente no. Muy corto tiempo
hace. Puede que haga dos o tres años. Una de las cosas más her-
mosas que yo ha visto. Hasta entre la familia pensaron que era
mentira.

De aquí de Alburquerque nos juimos un día viernes. Yo y mi
mujer. Saqué viernes y me juí, porque estábanos con las ganas de
matar carne. Ya hacía muncho tiempo que no habíanos matao
carne. Estaba con las ganas de jallar un novillo grande, un novillo
grande que tenía. No lo jallé pero jallé otro. Y lo encerré en el
corral que tiene Eduardo Valdez ai en la Mercé. Le dije a la mujer: "En la mañana vamos en la troca y lo traemos." Llegué a casa
oscuro ese viernes. Le di comida al caballo y la mujer me dio de
cenar a mí. Después de que me dio de cenar, pues naturalmente
me dieron ganas de ir al escusao.

Salí. ¡Nomás en cuento no la vide esta cosa muy extraña que
te digo! Cuando estaba sentao en el escusao, nomás en cuanto me
levanté y voy oyendo un ruido como una música y luego vide
una cosa tan hermosa, en la forma como de un cigarro, pero cosa
muy grande. Como la forma de un cigarro con una cola muy
larga. Los colores de la luz y la hermosura que era aquella cosa.
Lo mesmo que ver tú un *helicopter* que no tenga alas, pero con la
cola *muncho* más larga.

Hay un banco que le dicemos El Banco de la Cañada de la Máquina y La Cañada del Camino. Nosotros tamién tenemos, como
ustedes, una Cañada del Camino. Ése era el camino viejo, y loo
hay una máquina de trigo que hubo años pasaos, que la enterró
la agua ai, y de ai pa delante le quedó el nombre de El Banco de
la Cañada de la Máquina. Jue en ese banco onde bajó la cosa ésa.
Pero como te digo, esa cosa era en la forma de un cigarro, como
un tren, en la forma de un tren. Una cosa muy grande, muy
bonita. Y es un banco muy alto onde bajó. Bajó hasta que apla-

neó abajo de la cañada. Al llegar al arroyo, cuando aplaneó, se le acabó la luz de la cola, y adelante hizo una llama. De ai se despareció.

Con el mesmo ruido que hizo—yo le hablaba a mi mujer—y nomás en cuanto no la miró ella, porque ella se quedó lavando los trastes. Salió y tiró la agua.

—Ai bajó una fregaderas de esas—le dije—. Una fregaderas de esas. Ésas que dicen que andan ai en el viento.

Cuando yo truje la forma de la cosa aquí, a Alburquerque, con el mayordomo, le platiqué, y él me puso atención. Los otros dicían que yo mentía. El mayordomo me dijo:

—Ése era un UFO.

Yo ya le pinté la cosa asina.

—Píntemela—me dijo.

En un café estábanos, le estaba platicando. Le dije yo que estaba casi que ni la familia me creiba. La única que me cree es la mujer porque ella la vido. Porque cuando vine aquí a Alburquerque, vino mi hija a verme. Y estaba mi nieta. Yo platicándole a mi muchacha en español y a mi nieta en inglés. Y loo hasta ella, la muchacha, me dijo:

—Era un UFO *daddy*—me dijo. Era un UFO.

Y loo le dice mi hija a la muchachita, a la nieta:

—*Grandpa saw a UFO. That's what it is*—dijo—. *It's a UFO.*

Y el mayordomo me dijo tamién. Me dijo que ésa era un UFO.

—*Okay.* Pus vamos a ver—me dijo la nieta.

Fíjate tú, hasta la chamaca dudaba:

—*Come on grandpa! Come on, grandpa! Don't lie to us!*

Y loo le dije a mi nieta:

—Mira, te voy a dijir una cosa hijita. El *grandpa* no va a dijir una mentira a la familia, y asina no te va a dijir a ti—le dije.

—Yo quiero que me lleven—dijo—elotro sábado pa ver si la miro.

Pos yo ha visto cosas extrañas pero yo no sabía que esto era. "Pueda que no la mire, pero te voy a llevar."

—Mira apá. Eso está entre los dos nietos y tú—dijo mi hija,

porque dijieron que iban estar yendo al Cabezón hasta que vieran una.

Y cuando andaban, andaban jugando en el patio, ai detrás de la casa, haciéndose oscuro, cuando caminó una cosa semejante a la que vide yo pero más lejos. Pal rumbo de San Ysidro. Ai viene la cosa. Ella la chamaca jue la que la vido. ¡Y sí! Caminó. Venía pal lao de San Ysidro. La mesma cosa que la que había visto yo, pero *más* lejos. No tan cerquita. No oímos ruido ni nada de eso como yo; era muy lejos. Como pal rumbo de San Ysidro. ¡Pos pronto se despareció aquella cosa! Cuando de güenas a primeras se formó otra, en la forma de un güevo. Reluciente pero pal rumbo de Cuba. Y ai estamos con aquel azoro. La vieron ellos, los nietos. Tamién se despareció en el aigre.

¡Pero ésta te digo que despareció, cerquita, como tres cuartos de milla del Cabezón!

Si un día te enseño yo onde mero se despareció, dices tú, "No la vido lejos."

Strange Looking Objects

Benjamín "Benny" Lucero

And I've seen some strange things! At first I didn't. It's only been lately, perhaps in the last two or three years. One of the most beautiful things that I've ever seen. Even among the family, they thought it was a lie.

We left Albuquerque one day, on a Friday, my wife and I. I took Friday off and left, because we were in the mood for slaughtering an animal. It had been a long time since we'd slaughtered one. I was anxious to locate this large steer I had. I didn't find it but found another one instead and locked it up in a corral that Eduardo Valdez has there in La Merced. I said to my wife:

"Come morning we'll go in the truck and fetch it."

It was already dark that Friday, when I returned home. I fed the horse and my wife fixed supper for me. After she gave me something to eat, I felt like going to the bathroom.

I went out. I almost missed seeing this thing I'm telling you about. While in the outhouse, just as I got up to leave, I started to hear a music-like noise and then saw this beautiful object, shaped like a cigarette, but quite huge. It was shaped like a cigarette with a very long tail. The light, coupled with its colors, made that object so beautiful. It was like seeing a helicopter without wings, but with a much longer tail.

There's an embankment we call El Banco de la Cañada (The Cañada's Embankment) and La Cañada del Camino (The Road's Cañada). We also have, like you, a cañada called Cañada del Camino. That was the old road. Then there's a wheat threshing machine that was popular years ago, buried there by the water, whence the name El Banco de la Cañada de la Máquina. It was on that embankment where this object descended. But as I'm telling you, it was in the form of a cigarette, like a train, shaped like a train. A very huge and beautiful thing. And the embankment where this object came down is quite high. It descended until it was flat on the cañada. As it got to this arroyo, upon being even with the ground, the light on its tail disappeared, and the front-end of it spit out fire. From there it vanished completely.

Had it not been for the noise—I was telling my wife—she would have missed it, because she stayed back washing dishes. When she came out to toss the dishwater I said to her:

"One of those strange looking objects just came down. You know, one of those strange things that people claim can fly."

When I brought a drawing of the object here to Albuquerque, to my foreman, I talked to him about it, and he listened. The others said that I was lying. My foreman said to me:

"That was a UFO."

I proceeded to draw the thing for him.

"Draw it for me," he said.

We were in a cafe. I was telling him all about it. I was telling him that not even my family wanted to believe me. The only person who believes me is my wife because she saw it. After I had returned to Albuquerque, my daughter came to see me. And there was my granddaughter. I was talking to my daughter in Spanish, and to my granddaughter in English. And even she, my daughter, said to me:

"It was a UFO."

And then my daughter says to the little girl, my granddaughter:

"Grandpa saw a UFO. That's what it is," she said to her. "It's a UFO."

And my foreman told me the same thing. He said it was a UFO.

"Okay. Let's go see," said my granddaughter.

Imagine! Even the young squirt was skeptical:

"Come on grandpa! Come on, grandpa! Don't lie to us!"

Then I said to her:

"Listen. I'm going to tell you one thing. Grandpa's not going to tell the family a lie and, by the same token, he's not going to tell you one either," I said to her.

"I want you all to take me next Saturday," she said, "to see if I can see it."

Why I have seen strange objects but I didn't know that's what it was (a UFO).

"It's possible I won't see it, but I'm going to take you."

"Look here Dad. That's between you and your grandchildren," said my daughter, because the grandchildren said they would keep on going until they saw the object.

One time when they were playing in the patio, in the backyard, as it was beginning to get dark, suddenly an object similar to the one I had seen before went by, but farther away. In the direction of San Ysidro. There came the object. The granddaughter's the one who saw it. And sure enough! It moved right along. It was headed for San Ysidro. The same thing as what I had seen, but farther away. Not as close. We didn't hear a noise or anything like I did, but it was farther away, toward San Ysidro. Quickly that thing disappeared, when all of a sudden another one formed, in the shape of an egg. Glittering but toward Cuba. There we were in utter amazement. The grandchildren saw it. It, too, disappeared into space.

But this other one that I'm telling you about, it was really close, about three-fourths of a mile from Cabezón.

If some day I should show you the spot where it vanished, you'll say: "You weren't far from it."

La Ñeca

Emilia Padilla-García

Contaba un viejito, Benito, mi primo Benito, el que vivía al otro lao del Río Puerco, en el Arroyo de la Tapia que le dicen. Era músico. Y una noche jue a tocar a un baile, a Salazar. Güeno. Jue en un burro. Se acabó el baile. Agarró su violín el viejito éste y aquí viene por el camino. Por ai en el Arroyo de la Tapia, que está delante de en casa, ai brincó uno y se le subió anancas del burro. ¡Ora verás! Pues aquel hombre no jallaba qué hacer. "Quién eres tú, que pallá y que pacá," contaba muncho él. No, no le respondía. Pues aquí va aquel hombre embocándole al burro y aquel bulto anancas en el burro. No supo quién era; no supo. No supo. Él decía que no supo quién era.

Cuando llegó a la casa, al otro lao de casa, onde vivíanos nosotros, onde vivía la señá Juanita Salas . . . ¿Te acuerdas tú? Ai vivía su hija, señá Amada. Cuando llegó, es que llegó y se apeó y les grito a ellas: "Agárrenme, me vengo muriendo," y cayó destendido, desmayao. Es que le decían ellas: "¿Qué tiene papá? ¿Pus qué le dio?" "La Ñeca," es que decía. "La Ñeca." Que traiba la muñeca en el espinazo, pero ya no pudo hablar más. Eso era todo lo que decía.

Hasta otro día no les platicó de "La Ñeca" que se le había subido anancas del burro. Y lo *juraba* el dijunto Benito. Ya estaba viejito. Que era una muñeca, una mujer.

The Doll

Emilia Padilla-García

There was a little old man, who used to tell a story. Benito, my *primo* Benito, that was his name, who lived on the other side of the Río Puerco, a place known as El Arroyo de la Tapia (The Walled Arroyo). He was a musician. And one night he went to play at a dance in Salazar. Okay. He went on a donkey. The dance ended. This little old man then grabbed his violin and hit the road. At the Arroyo de la Tapia, or thereabouts, which is across from our house, "someone" jumped and climbed on the donkey's rump. Now, there's more to it! It seems the man, my primo Benito, was beside himself. He used to talk a lot about having asked, "Who are you?, this and that." No, why he never got an answer, all of which caused him to prompt his donkey, but that object still continued on the donkey's rump. He didn't find out who it was. He didn't; he just didn't. Don Benito simply said that he didn't know who it was.

When he got home, across from our house from where we used to live, where lady Juanita Salas lived. . . . Do you remember where? That's where her daughter, lady Amada lived. When he arrived, I understand he got home, climbed down from his donkey and hollered at them: "Catch me, I'm dying," and he fell flat on the floor. He had fainted. The ladies supposedly asked him: "What's wrong dad? What happened to you?" "The Doll," he'd answer. "The Doll." That he was carrying the doll on his back, but that was that. He was unable to speak anymore. All he could utter was "The Doll."

It wasn't until the following day that he spoke to them about "The Doll" that had climbed atop the donkey's rump. And the late Benito swore by it. He was already quite old. That it was a doll, a woman.

Un mono

Nasario P. García

Te voy a contar lo que en papá me platicaba. Posible que él estuviera joven toavía. Yo no estaba nacido en ese tiempo. Güeno, el cuento es que en papá me platicaba que él y sus amigos iban a los bailes en Salazar. Era, en ese tiempo, muy mentao. Hacían munchos bailes en ese lugar.

Había un hombre; él tocaba el violín. Y una noche venía de Salazar. No sé si vendría en un burro, o en una mula, pero no era caballo. Ai en un lugar que le dicen El Alto de los Jaramillos, ai venía este hombre solo. Cuando llegó en El Alto ese es que salió uno, como un mono, y se le subió en las anancas. El hombre se asustó muncho. El cuento es que cuando llegó a la casa, que, que, que vido la luz, se desmayŏ.

En ese Alto de los Jaramillos, según platicaba en papá, que es que ai salían munchas cosas. Eh, no brujas, pero como bultos y cosas asina.

A Rag Doll

Nasario P. García

I'm going to relate to you what my dad used to tell me. It's possible that he was still very young. I wasn't born yet. Nonetheless, the fact is that my dad used to tell me that he and friends of his would attend dances in Salazar. Back in those days Salazar was well known. They held many dances in that village.

There was a man, he played the violin, and one night he was on his way back from Salazar. I'm not sure whether he was riding a donkey, or a mule, but it wasn't a horse. At a place called El Alto de los Jaramillos, there was this man riding all alone. When he got to El Alto, someone emerged, like a rag doll, and it climbed on the donkey's rump. The man got terribly frightened. The fact is that when he got home, when he, he, he saw the kitchen light, he fainted.

On that Alto de los Jaramillos, according to what my dad talked about, many things supposedly appeared. Ah, not witches, but like objects, visions, and things like that.

Apareció un caballo

Nasario P. García

Y tamién es que venían una vez como dos o tres hombres, y éstos traiban sus güenos caballos y todo. Seguro que venían embolaos. De todos modos, me platicaba en papá que cuando iban por El Alto ése de los Jaramillos, es que ai se les apareció un caballo adelante de ellos. Loo es que dijo uno de ellos: "¿Y este caballo de diónde resultó?," es que les dijo. Pronto sacó su cabresto, lo amarró en la cabeza de la silla y es que gritó: "Yo lo lazo." Y le partió pero salió a juir el caballo. Pos lo alcanzó y lo lazó. Cuando los compañeros llegaron, él estaba caido par un lao y su caballo pal otro y el cabresto en el suelo, pero el caballo que había lazao no estaba.

Eso me platicaba en papá de los Moras. Asina se llamaban ellos; eran los Moras.

A Horse Popped Out

Nasario P. García

Another time I understand there were about two or three men and they were riding their best horses, saddles, and so forth. For sure they were drunk. Anyhow, my dad told me that when these men were crossing El Alto, named after the Jaramillos, a horse popped out of nowhere in front of them. Then one of them I guess said: "And where in the world did this horse come from?," so he said. No sooner said than done, he took out his rope, tied it to the saddle's horn, and hollered: "I'll rope it." And he took off after it, but the horse took off running. Well, he caught up with him and roped it. When his friends got there, he was to one side and his horse to the other, and the rope on the ground, but the horse which he had roped was no where in sight.

That's what my dad used to tell me about the Moras. That was their name, the Moras.

Chapter 5: The Supernatural

Un indio

Bencés Gabaldón

Mi papá nos platicaba a nosotros que hacían munchas cosas los indios ai en nuestro pais, y no sabía en qué manera podían hacelas. Unas cosas tan inteligentes que hacían estos indios.

Tenían un salón grande, y ai se rodeaban ellos a chupar y todo. Cantando. Onde estaban cantando, pues ai tiene usted que, que dicía él, mi papá, que ponían un cuero de cíbolo y lo tapaban y le ponían maiz abajo. Estaban cantando los indios y al rato que levantaban el cuero salían puros pollos, de abajo el cuero.

Y loo platicaba mi papá que se había subido este indio en un chivato, como en un filo de una sierra. Y estaba un voladero par un lao y el otro. Y ai es que iba poniendo el chivato las piernas entremedio y pasaba con él pal otro lao, y loo de allá pacá. Lo que no pudo hacer jue que la víbora, porque estaba una víbora para un lao, le metiera la lengua a él, porque cuando se arrimaba a onde estaba la víbora, en el pedimento de él, le pedía a Dios, ves, y no se arrimaba la víbora. Que se alzaba tan alta asina (dos o tres pies). No pudo. Nomás eso no pudo hacer la víbora, metele la lengua. De ai pallá hacía él todo. ¡Todo! Después lo que hacía él, lo hacía él siempre del mesmo modo.

Mi papá platicaba que era una barbaridá lo que hacían los indios; y él no sabía cómo. Eso nos platicó él a nosotros.

An Indian

Bencés Gabaldón

My father used to tell us that the Indians did many things there in our part of the country, but he didn't know in quite what way. The Indians performed such intelligent feats!

They had a huge room and that's where they gathered around to smoke and all that sort of thing. They did so by singing. Wherever they were singing, you understand, according to my father, they'd put a bison's hide, cover it, and put corn underneath.

And then my father also used to talk about this Indian who had mounted a billy goat on a mountain ridge. There was a precipice to one side as well as to the other. And I understand that it was on that ridge that the billy goat walked gingerly, first to one end and then to the other, with the Indian on its back. Oh, another thing, what the billy goat did not succeed in doing, because there was a snake to one side, was to allow the snake to strike the Indian. The reason that did not happen was that whenever he came close to the snake, due to his petition to God, it did not strike him. The snake supposedly raised itself so high, about two or three feet in the air, but it failed in its attempt to strike. That's the only thing the snake was unable to do—to bite him. Other than that, the Indian did everything at will. I mean everything! Anytime he did something, he always did it the same way.

My father would say that it was really something the kinds of things the Indians could perform. He simply didn't know how they did it. That was his story to us.

Chapter 5: The Supernatural

Brujerías

Salomón Lovato

Lo que sí se vían más aá eran brujerías. Yo nomás una vez me tocó ver. No brujerías. Lo que vide jue luces en el camino. Es todo. Pero yo no creibo; no creibo nada en eso. Porque a mí se me hace que la brujería es la gente que está viva que hace mal a la gente que está viva. No es la gente que está muerta que hace mal a la gente que está viva. Es al revés. Pero hay munchos toavía—usted habrá leido—que hay munchos modos de hacer, de hacer *hocus-pocus* y lo que sea. Y yo creo que eso era pero la gente se creiba muncho en brujerías.

Se enfermaba un hombre o una mujer: "Le hicieron mal a mi marido." "¿Vites que andaba bailando con aquélla?" Pero eso no era en mi tiempo. Yo oí eso de los viejitos.

Me tocó ver una vez este cierto hombre, que me da escalofrío toavía cuando me acuerdo. Vine con mi agüelito pacá pa Bernalillo. Estaba una, ¿cómo le decían?, *sujarana, sujarana*, le decían, de esas gentes que curan brujerías. Y este hombre lo trujieron ai porque tenía, que tenía, ah, le tenían hecho mal o no sé qué. Y vine yo; yo estaba mediano. Porque yo anduve muncho con mi agüelo, por lao de en papá. Me quería muncho. Él estaba solo; no tenía esposa. Mi agüela se murió; yo ni la conocí. De manera que yo era su compañero. Y él era pariente de este hombre.

Vinimos pa Bernalillo de San Luis y jueron y vieron esta señora. Yo me acuerdo que entramos a una casa que tenía un fogón de campana. Y loo tenía un cajete con hierbas. ¡Y el apeste! ¡El olor era terrible! Yo no me fijé. No me importaba. Tenía lumbre. Había muncha gente. Y estaba esta señora ai; no sé qué estaría haciendo, rezando o qué, no importa qué estuviera haciendo. Y loo cuando menos acordé, dice:

—¡Miren aquí está—dijo—. Éste es el que le tiene hecho mal a usted. Un indio—dijo.

Y todos jueron aá a ver (la imagen en el cajete de hierbas). Yo no vide nada. No había nada.

Witchcraft

Salomón Lovato

What one really saw a lot of over in San Luis was witchcraft. I only got to see it once. Not sorceries. What I saw were lights on the road. That's all. But I don't believe in any of that stuff, because I believe that sorcery is people themselves who inflict harm on other people who are also living. It's not the dead who do harm to those who are alive. It's the other way around. But there are still many—perhaps you've heard—many ways of doing hocus-pocus or whatever. I believe that that's what it was, but people believed a lot in witchcraft.

Let us say that a man or a woman became ill: "Someone did something evil to my husband." "Did you see him dancing with that woman?" But that wasn't during my time. I heard that from the old-timers.

Once I had the opportunity of seeing this man, which still brings chills up and down my spine when I think about it. I came over here to Bernalillo with my grandfather. There was a, what do you call her? A *sujarana*, a *sujarana*, that's what they called her, one of those persons who treats sorcery. And they brought this man to this lady because someone had done something evil to him or what have you. And I came along; I was very small. You see, I did a lot of traveling with my grandfather, on my father's side. He liked me a lot. He lived alone; he didn't have a wife. My grandma had died; I didn't even know her. So that, in a way, I was his companion. And he was a relative of this man.

We came to Bernalillo from San Luis, and they went and saw this woman. I remember that we entered this house that had a kitchen fireplace with a hood. And she had a tub full of weeds. And the stench was something else! The smell was terrible! I didn't care. It didn't bother me. The lady had a fire going. There were lots of people. And there she was. I don't know what she was doing, praying or what. It doesn't matter what she was doing. And all of a sudden when I least expected it, she said:

"Look! Here he is," she said. "This is the one who's caused you evil. It's an Indian," she said.

Everybody went over there to see (the Indian's image in the bathtub). I didn't see anything. There was nothing.

Chapter 5: The Supernatural

Brujerías navajosas

Benjamín "Benny" Lucero

Este compadre mío, Emilio, me platicaba a mí que entre los nava-joses hacen males. Me platicaba historias, lo que pasó en un indi-viduo navajó, que tenía a su papá, y su papá de él era brujo.

De Torreón al Pueblo del Alto es muy lejos, y estos brujos no importa que tan lejos esté una fiesta; agarran un caballo, lo caminan, y van. Iban en aquellos años de a caballo, y es que le dijo: "¡Oh!," es que le dijo el papá al hijo, "orita te llevo a esa fiesta, pero nos vamos a tener que venir antes de media noche." Cuando llegaron, es que llegaron dos coyotes. Esto le platicaba el muchacho éste, el hijo, a mi compadre. Cien años tiene ora. Salió esa confianza, ¿ves? Y me dijo que es que le había platicao el muchacho que habían llegao hechos dos coyotes: uno jue el papá y el otro jue él mesmo. Antes de medianoche, porque después de medianoche no pueden andar los brujos. Cuando se llegó la medianoche, estuvieron en la fiesta, cuando ya se llegó la media-noche me arrendé patrás, es que le dijo el hijo. Ai es que le dijo a su papá que no quería nada con él. ¡No más! Su papá era brujo. Y oí yo mentar mucho eso entre los navajoses, que sabía el hijo que dijían que su papá es que era brujo.

Navajo Witchcraft

Benjamín "Benny" Lucero

Emilio, this compadre of mine, used to tell me that the Navajos inflict evil on one another. He'd tell me stories, like what happened to a particular Navajo, whose father was still living and was a witch.

From Torreón to El Pueblo del Alto is quite a ways, but for witches distance is a relative thing when it comes to a party; they grab a horse, ride it, and go. Back in those days they rode on horseback, and the father supposedly said to the son: "Oh, I'll take you to that party in a little bit, but we'll have to return before midnight." When the two arrived, it was in the form of two coyotes. That's what this fellow, the Navajo's son, used to tell my compadre. My compadre's one-hundred years old now. You see, confidence was at hand. And he told me that the boy had confided in him that he and his father arrived having turned into coyotes: he one and his father the other. This happened before midnight because after twelve midnight the witches can't be roaming around. When midnight came, because they had already been at the party, when midnight approached I went back, so said the son to my compadre. He told his father that from then on he didn't want anything to do with him. Nothing more! His father was a witch. And I overheard that a lot among the Navajos; that is, the son knew that they supposedly spoke of his father of being a witch.

Es que era navajosa

Benjamín "Benny" Lucero

Había un gringo que vino en estos últimos años, que nosotros le cambiamos las cabras por vacas, y este gringo le andaba dando güelta a las vacas que estaban ai. Y éste le partió a un coyote, pero éste sí se acobardó. Brincó el coyote pa bajo del arroyo y el gringo agarró una vereda asina par un lao y vido que estaba una navajosa atrincada, contra el barranco cobijada con un tápalo. Cuando bajó abajo, se cambió . . . y es que era navajosa.

Eso es que platicó este gringo que estaba en la tienda del lugar, como te digo, porque mi compadre Emilio, que tenía *muy* güen inglés, lo escuchó.

Se golvió navajó

Benjamín "Benny" Lucero

Pero también me platicaba asina otro caso semejante mi compadre Emilio. Es que un navajó le partió a un coyote, y este navajó sí traiba rifle. Y a la güelta de un sabino, que ya iba pa pisotear el coyote éste que pensaba que andaba haciendo mal a las borregas, éste sí traiba rifle, y a la güelta de un sabino, estaba un navajó. Se golvió un navajó. De coyote se golvió a navajó. Se cansó, seguro, ¿ves? Y es que le dicía el navajó: "No me mates, hombre. No me mates," cuando el mesmo brujo, el navajó, se soltó con una flecha, nomás que pegó en la silla abajo, la flecha. Pero la flecha estaba clavada. Y a este navajó sí es que sacó el rifle y le dio. Eso sí me platicaba mi compadre Emilio.

Es que estaba con un tápalo: "No me mates. No me mates," es que le dicía, porque traiba rifle él. Que le estaba diciendo él que si pa qué hacía esas cosas y el brujo es que le dicía: "No. No me mates. No me mates," es que le dijo, cuando el chillido de la flecha pegó abajo en la montura. Le jerró.

A Coyote Turned Woman

Benjamín "Benny" Lucero

There was a gringo, with whom we traded goats for cows, who
migrated to the Río Puerco Valley in the last few years, and he
was checking up on the cows that he had there. He took off after a coyote, but the latter chickened out. The coyote jumped
to the bottom of the arroyo and the gringo took off on a trail to
one side and there at the bottom spotted a Navajo woman, up
against a river bank, covered with a shawl. When she climbed
down, she turned into . . . she was a woman.

That's what this gringo who was in the local grocery store
talked about, as I say, because my compadre Emilio, who understood English *very* well, overheard him.

A Coyote Turned Navajo

Benjamín "Benny" Lucero

But then again my compadre Emilio used to tell me about another similar case. It seems a Navajo took off after a coyote, and
he did have a rifle. As he went around this juniper, about to step
on this coyote, whom he thought was doing damage to his
sheep, and as he went around the juniper, there was a Navajo.
The coyote turned into a Navajo. You see, he must have gotten
tired of running. The coyote-turned Navajo would tell the
Navajo. "Man, don't kill me. Don't kill me," when the witch
himself, the Navajo, let go with an arrow. The only thing is that
the arrow hit the lower part of the saddle. But there was the arrow, stuck. For this particular coyote-turned Navajo the Navajo
did pull out his rifle and struck him with it. That's one thing my
compadre used to tell me.

There it was, the coyote-turned Navajo, with a shawl: "Don't kill me. Don't kill me," so he begged because the Navajo had a rifle. The Navajo was asking him why he did those things and the witch would merely respond: "No. Don't kill me. Don't kill me," when suddenly the shrilling sound of an arrow . . . breezed by the mount. The arrow missed him.

La peyotera

Benjamín "Benny" Lucero

Me acuerdo de que dicía en papá que él tenía un pariente, un primo. La mujer de este pariente nomás lo vía—porque en papá era un hombre muy pesao, en un modo, era muy corajudo—y es que le dijía ella: "¿Sabes tú?," es que le dijía a en papá. "Tú eres un hombre muy pesao. A ti no te pueden hacer mal los brujos."

Y dijía en papá que este primo estaba casao con una mujer que sabía hacer males. Eran males. "Yo soy quien soy," le dicía a en papá. Él platicaba que "nomás me vía esa mujer y arrancaba. Nomás no me podía ver. Era peyotera; sabía hacer males." Es que tienen cierto tiempo los brujos, que hacen mal.

En una vez es que llegó en papá a caballo a ver a su primo, ya cuando pasaron munchos años. Y es que le dijo ella: "¡Ándale! ¡Corre!" Quiso decile: "No soy bruja. "¡Ya no soy bruja!" es que le dijo. "¡Ándale! ¡Corre! ¡Ya no soy bruja!"

Asina dicía en papá que la mujer sabía hacer mal. "Pero no me arrimé a comer," dijo. "Me quedé mirándola. Nomás me quedé mirándola, y asina pasó," dijo.

The Peyote Lady

Benjamín "Benny" Lucero

I remember my dad saying that he had a relative, a cousin. All this relative's wife had to do was look at him—because my dad was a very thick skinned man and, in a way, very temperamental—and she'd say to him: "Do you know," she'd say to him, "that you're a very thick skinned man? Not even witches can inflict harm on you."

And he'd say that this cousin was married to a woman who was capable of sorcery. Evil doings. "I am who I am," she'd say to my dad. He used to say that "no sooner she'd see me and she'd take off. She just couldn't stand the sight of me. She was a peyote woman; she was versed in inflicting evil." I understand witches can inflict harm only at a given time.

Once upon a time, many years later, my dad arrived on horseback to see his cousin, and his wife said to him: "Come on now! Come!" She tried to say: "I'm no witch. I'm no longer one. Come on now! Come! I'm no longer a witch!"

Why dad swore that the woman was capable of doing people harm. "But I didn't sit down to eat," he said. "I stayed staring at her. I just stayed looking at her, and that's the way it happened."

Aquella viejita

Bencés Gabaldón

Otra vez me acuerdo yo un hermano mío, y un primo hermano mío tamién; ellos venían de Cabezón. Y había una viejita; tenía un cuartito en un lao del camino. Ai vivía. Y cuando venían de allá ellos pacá, pus ya serían como las doce de la noche: por ai una cosa asina, las diez, una cosa asina. Cuando iban pasando estaba aquella viejita nomás escarbando la ceniza onde tiraba la basura uno. ¡Sepa Dios! Y loo de ai ya no se vido. La vieron ellos. Eso sí lo sé yo porque ellos me platicaron.

Le sacó un ojo al gato

Bencés Gabaldón

Nos platicaba mamá a nosotros que una vez esta mujer . . . pues, eh, estaban en una casa. En esos tiempos la gente se juntaba, quizás, yo no sé, se juntaba la gente en una casa y se ponían a hacer lonche en la noche. A comer y eso. Y entró una de las mujeres, es que entró, pa la dispensa pa sacar, pa sacar, no sé qué iría a trae, iba a trae alguna cosa de la dispensa, y cuando menos pensó se le vino un gato encima a ella y le pegó ella. No sé con qué le dio y le sacó un ojo al gato. Y el gato voló y se jue y no lo agarraron.

Otro día no era el gato; era una mujer. Era una mujer la que andaba. Y loo decían que se había sacao el ojo en una armella, de la puerta. Pero jue el garrotazo del gato.

Pa que veiga usted lo que son las cosas. ¡Esas cosas pasaban!

That Little Old Lady

Bencés Gabaldón

I remember another time a brother of mine and a cousin were also coming from Cabezón. And there was this little old lady; she had a little shack next to the road. That's where she lived. And when my brother and cousin were headed home to San Luis from Cabezón, well, it must have been about twelve o'clock at night, somewhere around there, ten o'clock, something like that. When they approached the little old lady's house there she was digging up the ashes where one dumped the trash. God knows what she was doing! And then she disappeared, but they saw her for sure. That I know because they told me so.

The Cat Lost An Eye

Bencés Gabaldón

My mom used to tell us that once upon a time this woman . . . well, ah, they were in this certain home. Back in those days the people got together, I understand, I don't know, in someone's home and they fixed snacks at night. To eat and that sort of thing. And one of the ladies entered, supposedly, the pantry to fetch, to fetch, I don't know what she was going to get, something from the pantry, when all of a sudden a cat leaped at her and she hit it. I don't know what she hit the cat with, but she put out one of his eyes. The cat took off flying and left and wasn't caught.

On the following day people found out that it wasn't a cat. It was a woman; it was a woman who was snooping around. And then everyone went about saying that she had lost her eye on a door's lock, but it was the blow she received instead that caused it.

See what things are like! Those things used to go on.

Dos brujas y dos juanes

Nasario P. García

Mi agüelo se llamaba Juan García, su papá de en papá, y estaba
cieguito. Y él venía de allá de Gualupe pacá pa La Plaza, pa Alburquerque. Yo no sé con quiénes vendría él, o a qué vendría. Yo no
sé si a llevar provisiones. Yo no sé, pero ai en La Ceja, onde estaban campeando—era en el mes de mayo—vieron, vieron
venir dos luces. Iban de aquí de Alburquerque. Y loo empezaron
a platicar él y sus otros compañeros, y venía *otro* Juan tamién,
amás de mi agüelo. Y loo es que les preguntó mi agüelo que si de
qué rumbo venían las luces. Ya le dijieron. "Pues, llévame," es
que le dijo mi agüelo a en papá, y se jueron los dos juanes, lejos
de dionde tenían el campo. Ai es que hicieron una raya los
juanes pal rumbo que venían las dos luces. Hicieron una raya con
una rueda, una aquí y otra allá, una pa cada luz. Loo se quitaron,
sí, se quitaron, la camiseta y la pusieron en cada rueda y se
jueron patrás pal campo. Cuando de güenas a primeras aquí van
las luces y se desparecieron. Al rato vinieron mi agüelo y el otro
Juan a ver y es que ai estaban cobijadas dos mujeres con las
camisetas que dejaron los juanes.

Tengo entendido que éstas eran dos mujeres que iban pa La
Sierra del Valle, que le llaman, par onde estaban sus maridos en la
borrega tresquilando. Es que las mujeres eran de aquí de Los Duranes o de Los Griegos en Alburquerque; o no sé diónde dijo en
papá. Eso sí me platicaba en papá.

¡Pues eran brujas! ¡Brujas! ¡Qué pueden haber sido! Estas brujas
iban volando, ¿ves?, pero aquellos, los juanes, pueden agarrar las
brujas, si saben. ¿Entiendes? Los juanes tienen muncho poder si
saben pa agarrar las brujas. Tocó que en esa oportunidá había dos
juanes.

Pues, eh, es que ellas les dijieron a ellos que iban pa La Sierra
del Valle, par onde estaban sus maridos, que estaban en la tres-
quila. Antonces ellas les ofrecían no sé qué tantas cabras nomás

porque las soltaran. Las soltaron. Y se levantaron ellas y se jueron. Volando. Pero reclaman, yo no sé en qué modo lo harán, que pueden salir pa juera y ai mesmo pueden volverse como un pájaro y volar. Eso sí me platicaba en papá.

Two Witches and Two Fellows Named John

Nasario P. García

My paternal grandfather's name was Juan García, and was blind.
He was on his way from Guadalupe to town, to Albuquerque. I
don't know whom he could have been coming with, or the purpose of the trip. I don't know if it was to take groceries back to
the ranch. I just don't know, but there in La Ceja (The Summit),
where they were camping—it was during the month of May—
they saw two lights coming. The lights were headed from here
in Albuquerque. And then he and his other buddies began to
chitchat. In addition, there was another Juan, besides my grandfather. And then I understand my grandfather asked them which
direction the lights were coming from, so they told him. "Well,
take me," my grandfather supposedly said to my dad, and the
two fellows named John took off, far from where their camp
was. There they made a line in the direction of the lights. The
mark was in the form of a circle, one in one place and another in
another, one for each light. Then each Juan took off, yes, each
one took off his undershirt and put it in each circle and returned
to their campsite. When all-of-a-sudden here go the lights; they
disappeared. A little while later my grandfather and the other
fellow named John returned to see and there were the two
women covered with the two undershirts that my grandfather
and the other Juan had left.

I understand that these two women were on their way to La
Sierra del Valle (The Mountain of the Valley), as it's called, where
their husbands were shearing sheep. The women supposedly
were from Los Duranes (The Durans) or Los Griegos (The Griegos)
in Albuquerque; or I don't know where my dad said they were
from. That's what my dad used to tell me.

Well, they were witches! Witches! What else could they have
been! These witches were airborne, you see, but those fellows

named John, they're capable of catching them, provided they know how. Do you understand? The *juanes* have a lot of power if they know how to catch witches. It so happened that on that occasion there were two *juanes*.

Well, the women presumably told them that they were headed for La Sierra del Valle, where their husbands were, who were involved in shearing sheep. Then the witches offered the two *juanes* I don't know how many goats if they would just turn them loose. They did so. And they rose and took off. Flying. But people claim that the witches are able to go outside and right there they can turn into a bird and fly. I don't know how they manage it. That for sure my dad used to tell me.

Una palmazón

Bencés Gabaldón

En otra vez—ésta es otra clase de negocio—un tío mío es que estaba cortando trigo. Güeno. Y luego había, tú sabes lo que es una sociedá. Es la Sociedá de Nuestro Padre Jesús. Y empezó un hombre a darse azotes con las espigas de trigo. Es que le dijieron: "¿Pa qué estás haciendo eso hombre?", haciéndose azotes como los Penitentes. "Mira," es que dijo otro, "te va a castigar mi Tata Dios por eso." "Te va a castigar," es que le dijo uno de ellos. "Te va a castigar."

Güeno. No creyó él. Con el tiempo le salió una palmazón aquí en el espinazo. Una palmazón en el espinazo. Tuvo que entrar a la sociedá él pa que se le quitara eso que él había producido, lo que había hecho él. Andaba buslándose de ellos, de los Penitentes, y le salió esa palmazón. Ya no vivía, estaba muriéndose. Nomás entró a la sociedá y se le quitó todo. Ya no volvió él a mover nada de eso.

¿Ves? Son cosas que pasan ésas, y no es mentira. Esas cosas pasaron. ¡Y pasan! Por eso no sirve hacer uno eso. Esa clase de negocio, mira, de querer uno, de querer uno buslarse de otro, no pasa. No pasa. Eso le hace mal a uno mesmo. ¿Qué no?

Esto es lo que me acuerdo yo. Es como nos platicaban a nosotros. Pero munchas cosas . . . cosas que no sabe uno ni cómo andan ni cómo caminan ni nada. En ese lugar, el Río Puerco, había brasas y eso. Nosotros las vimos. Yo las llegué a ver. No es que me platicaran a mí. Yo las vide.

A Huge Palm-Like Growth

Bencés Gabaldón

On another occasion—this has to do with something else—the story goes that an uncle of mine was cutting wheat. Okay. And then there was, you know what a fraternity is? It was the Fraternity of Our Lord Jesus Christ. Anyway, a man began to whip himself with wheat tassels. I understand the brothers admonished him: "Why are you doing that, my dear man?," because he was feigning that he was beating himself like the Penitente Brothers. "Listen," interjected another one of the brothers, "the Good Lord is going to punish you for that. He's going to punish you." "He's going to punish you," echoed another one of the Penitentes present.

Well, so much for that. The man didn't believe any of them. It wasn't long before this man developed a huge palm-like growth right on his back. A huge palm-like growth on his back. He had to join the brotherhood in order to get rid of that thing which he had brought upon himself, because of what he had done. He went around making fun of the Penitente Brothers, and that's why he got that huge palm-like growth. His days were numbered; he was dying. No sooner he joined the fraternity and the huge palm-like growth disappeared. And that was the last time he messed around with that kind of thing.

You see, these are things that went on. That's no lie. Those things used to go on. And they still do! That's why it's wise not to get involved in those kinds of things. You see, that kind of business, of wanting to mock someone else, doesn't pay. It just doesn't pay. You only harm yourself. Don't you agree?

That's what I remember about that incident. That's what we were told. But many things, things that one is unaware of, or how they happened or came about, used to go on in that part of the world called the Río Puerco. These flying red sparks and all of that, we saw them. I got to see them. It's not that somebody told me about them. I saw them myself.

Narrators: Biographical Sketches

Narrators: Biographical Sketches

Juan Armijo was born north of Guadalupe, New Mexico on the Río Puerco in 1902 and died in Old Town in Albuquerque on July 18, 1984. His family lived in El Vallecito de los Navajoses where the Arroyo Chico and the Río Puerco come together, a short distance from the village of Guadalupe. El Vallecito de los Navajoses was considered part of Guadalupe; it was there where he spent his first years until reaching adulthood. In 1931 he married Susanita Ramírez in Jémez, known years ago as La Misión de San Diego de Jémez to which people of Guadalupe, Casa Salazar, Cabezón, and San Luis belonged. About five months after being married he and his wife moved to San Ysidro, New Mexico, close to Jémez. Later they moved to Albuquerque. It was here that they raised their children. He lived quietly with his wife in Old Town until his death.

Susanita Ramírez de Armijo was born in Guadalupe, New Mexico, in 1916. She, like her husband Juan Armijo, also spent her early childhood and adolescence in El Valle de los Navajoses close to Guadalupe until 1931 when they were married in Jémez at La Misión de San Diego de Jeméz. Once they were married they returned to Guadalupe, but their stay was short-lived. Five months later Susanita and Juan Armijo moved to San Ysidro, New Mexico, a small community not far from Bernalillo and Albuquerque.

Susanita, like many of her fellow compatriots from the Río Puerco Valley, is extremely religious. In a special room at home in Old Town in Albuquerque she has her favorite santos, but, more importantly, she is very proud of her *corte celestial* (saints and angels in heaven according to the Catholic faith). This is where she does most of her praying instead of going to the church on the plaza.

Juan Armijo and Susanita Ramírez de Armijo

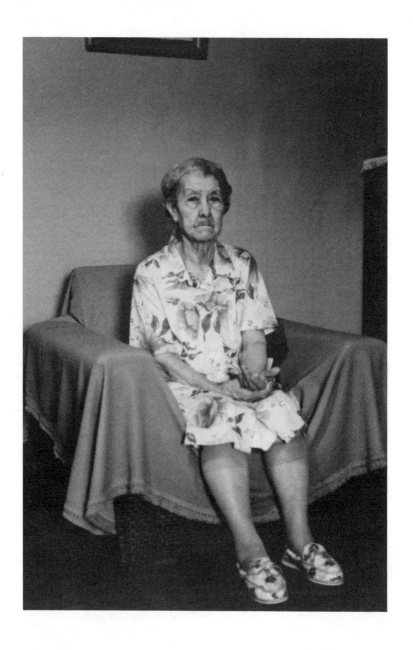

Narrators: Biographical Sketches

Perfilia Córdova lived nearly one hundred years. She was born in Guadalupe on January 22, 1890 in the territory of New Mexico. She and her family did not live in the village of Guadalupe *per se* where the church, oratory and school were, but rather across the Río Puerco, about a mile from the placita. In 1911, at twenty-one years of age, she married Jesús Córdova. Both of them continued residing in Guadalupe, earning a living as ranchers, like so many of their neighbors and relatives, until he was drafted into the United States Army after World War I broke out. Meanwhile, she remained in Guadalupe, living with her family. In 1917 he returned with a maimed right arm from an injury that he suffered in the war. He and his wife were forced to leave Guadalupe that same year. They moved to Bernalillo, where she lived with an only daughter after the death of her husband. She died February 27, 1987.

Perfilia Córdova

Narrators: Biographical Sketches

Adrián Chávez, even though he was born in Armijo, southwest of Albuquerque (today considered part of Albuquerque), on the 15th of December, 1913, lived in Guadalupe with his stepparents, Natividad Gutiérrez de Romero, and Paz Romero, from the time he was very young. His father ran a store and was a bootlegger.

His real father, Miguel Chávez, was from Los Chávez, situated between Belén and Los Lunas. Teresa Armijo, his mother's family, was from Armijo. Adrián Chávez claims that his paternal grandparents, José and Demetria Chávez, came from Spain, but he was not sure if his maternal grandparents, Luis Armijo y Josefa Lovato, were also of Spanish stock.

Today Adrián Chávez owns only a few "patches" of property in El Coruco, near Guadalupe, that he inherited from his stepfather, but he rarely visits his former home since abandoning it in 1941 (he lived there from 1926 until 1941). His wife Vicentita Chávez, was also born in Guadalupe.

Adrián Chávez and Vicentita Chávez

Bencés Gabaldón, the son of Basilio Gabaldón and Abrahana, was born on May 12, 1894 in San Luis, New Mexico. His parents were born in Algodones, about twenty-five miles north of Albuquerque. Later they went to San Luis, a small village on the Río Puerco named in honor of Louis IX, king of France in the XIII century. In years past San Luis was known as La Tijera (The Scissors).

Bencés Gabaldón's first wife died in San Luis; he remarried in 1929, this time to Mary, with whom he lives in Bernalillo today. They abandoned San Luis for good in 1963.

In spite of his age, he is in good health. He even drives his truck daily to the post office to pick up his mail. He remembers his past with marvelous clarity and talks about it with enthusiasm and emotion.

In Bernalillo he is known as one of the best *rezadores* (a person renowned for his/her praying ability) and singer of hymns of praise (*alabados*). Before our interview ended, he sang a sad and emotional hymn; tears flowed down his cheeks, as he recited the last verse.

Bencés Gabaldón

Narrators: Biographical Sketches

Nasario P. García, son of Teodoro José García and Emilia Padilla, was born in El Rincón del Cochino (The Hog's Corner) between Guadalupe and Casa Salazar on the 10th of September, 1912. As a young man he turned cowboy, sacrificing his education. In 1934 his father, somewhat political, got him a job as a janitor at the Court House in Bernalillo. Here he met Agapita López, from San Miguel, a tiny village close to Cuba, and married her in 1935. In Guadalupe they tried to eke out a living by farming and raising animals, but it was difficult for them once they started to have children. In 1944 they gave up and left for Albuquerque, where he worked for twenty-eight years for Crane O'fallon Company. He retired in 1972, the same year his wife and parents died.

Today he lives alone in Los Ranchos de Albuquerque. He visits Guadalupe quite frequently because he still owns property and a few head of cattle.

Nasario P. García

Narrators: Biographical Sketches

Adelita Gonzales was born on June 11, 1909 in Guadalupe, New Mexico. Almost fifty years later, in 1958, she and her children had to leave the village because Sandoval County could no longer provide them with a school teacher.

At that time Adelita Gonzales, the wife of Salvador, was in charge of a small grocery store (where the post office was located) owned by Élfego Aranda from Albuquerque. The Gonzaleses represented the last breath of hope in Guadalupe because without them the only thing that was left were memories and empty houses which became targets for looters with a penchant for destruction.

Adelita Gonzales was always famous—and still is in Albuquerque where she lives—for being a great *rezadora* (renowned for her praying ability and singer of hymns of praise [*alabados*]). Few can surpass her in this endeavor.

Adelita Gonzales is an extraordinary person who sees her past as well as her future in a very clear way and harbors no bitterness toward anyone.

Adelita Gonzales

Edumenio (Ed) Lovato, who now lives in Albuquerque, was born on the 12th of February in 1913 in San Luis, New Mexico. His parents were Feliz Lovato, born in San Luis, and Florinda Jaramillo, from Casa Salazar.

Edumenio Lovato suffered from polio when he was a child and still limps as he walks. He never married; instead he cared for his parents while they were alive. Today his youngest brother takes care of cattle that he (Ed) owns in San Luis on land inherited from his father.

Of all the persons interviewed for this collection of stories, Edumenio Lovato is the only one who ever attended the university. He is bilingual and writes and speaks in English as well as in Spanish. Throughout the years he has maintained an interest in the history of the Río Puerco Valley and the folklore belonging to its people.

Edumenio "Ed" Lovato

Salomón (Sal) Lovato, Edumenio's brother, was also born in San Luis, New Mexico, on the 4th of April, 1915. In 1936 he married Laura Tachías from Cabezón, whose father Rendolfo Tachías supposedly was from Puerto Rico. Laura Tachías's mother was Adelaida Sandoval, who belonged to the Sandovals, a prominent family in Sandoval County for whom the county was named.

In 1945, after serving in the United States Army, Salomón Lovato returned to his birthplace where he continued to fight for the rights of ranchers, especially since many people complained about the government's injustices that were being carried out under the Taylor Grazing Act of 1934. In 1966 Salomón Lovato finally sold his ranch in San Luis. Today he is retired from the government, for which he worked many years. His first wife died in 1973, but he has since remarried.

Salomón "Sal" Lovato

Benjamín "Benny" Lucero

Benjamín Lucero, known as Benny since he was a child, was born in Cabezón, New Mexico on June 29, 1924. Benjamín was the name given him by his baptismal godparents. Benny Lucero's parents were Clemente, born in Cabezón, and Clara Lucero de Lucero, from Corrales. In 1945 Benny Lucero married Egripina (Tina) Lovato, from San Luis, in Albuquerque.

In 1952 or 1953 the Luceros left for Albuquerque, where the two of them still reside today. Nevertheless, he has never completely given up Cabezón. As he said: "But I still go all the time. I come and go. I live over there on Saturdays and Sundays." Not only does he own cattle and property but he is also the principal owner of Cabezón. Around 1964 strangers or outsiders started to go into Cabezón to vandalize and cause looting. Benny Lucero and other Cabezón landowners complained to Sandoval County, and finally the commissioners ordered Cabezón closed to the public. It was then that Benny Lucero put a fence around the village so that people would no longer trespass and cause destruction.

Emilia Padilla García. Photograph provided by author.

Narrators: Biographical Sketches

Emilia Padilla-García was born about 1885 in Pecos, New Mexico in San Miguel County. Her father, Antonio Padilla, worked for the railroad, where he died in an accident when she was eight years old. She was left an orphan because her mother was already deceased, so relatives took her to live with one of her grandmothers in Corrales, northwest of Albuquerque. Her grandmother died soon thereafter.

In 1897, at twelve years of age, Emilia Padilla left for Casa Salazar to live with an aunt. There she met Teodoro José García who had gone there with his father from Algodones in 1880 at eight years of age.

Emilia Padilla and he were married in 1898 in Casa Salazar. Through the Homestead Act of 1862 Emilia Padilla and her husband purchased their first property and built a home in Guadalupe. They raised many crops, cattle, horses, goats and pigs, but eventually succumbed to lack of water and misfortune.

Both of them died in Albuquerque in 1972: he was one hundred years old; she was about eighty-eight.

Narrators: Biographical Sketches

Damiano Romero, a Casa Salazar native, was born there on June 4, 1916, and died on February 22, 1984. He is one of few ranchers who earned a living raising cattle in the Río Puerco Valley. "I have lived all of my life over there. That's where I stay . . . and if they should toss me out from over there it would be like killing me."

Damiano Romero talked of a kind of a slow death that the government had imposed on him and other ranchers. He complained in this fashion: "As I have said to many people, especially to officials of the government, I have lost my rights. I have lost everything." As a result he saw his life in a philosophical and even cynical way: "When I was twenty years old, I valued my life like gold. When I reached thirty, it was like silver. When I got to forty, it was like copper. At age fifty, it turned to tin. And now I'm sixty-two years old, and now my life is worth less."

He maintained two homes, including one in Los Ranchos de Albuquerque where his wife Virginia still lives.

Damiano Romero

Cleofas Salas, Alberto Salas

Narrators: Biographical Sketches

Alberto Salas was born May 10, 1909 in Guadalupe. Today he spends his days quietly with his wife Cleofas in Los Ranchos de Albuquerque. He lived in Guadalupe until 1949, one year after his father Crescencio Salas died. Alberto Salas spoke about Guadalupe with joy, sadness and bitterness. What he misses most is the good times with his parents. He also recalled the freedom once enjoyed by farmers because, as he said, "When one works for oneself, there's nobody pricking your ribs, because here in places like Albuquerque, it's the clock that makes us be on the run." His contempt is due principally to the government's abuse and injustices against the ranchers.

In spite of these sad memories, he and his wife take their sons and daughters and grandchildren to Guadalupe to educate them about a past laden with harsh but pleasant memories.

Luciano Sánchez, who comes from a family of folk healers, was born in Guadalupe, New Mexico, on July 12, 1910, where he resided until 1943. Until his wife Reyitos died in 1985 they both lived in Los Griegos de Albuquerque. The two of them would visit Guadalupe once in a while because he still owns property that his father, José Sánchez, left him.

What Luciano Sánchez recalls more than anything about Guadalupe is the respect and kindness that prevailed among all the people. "Why I remember," he says, "over there everyone was like related. We called everyone, even if they were not blood related, we referred to them as my uncle, my cousin, . . ." Since there were poor families, one would help the other. If a cow was slaughtered in the village, "that day turned out to be very special because all of the neighbors, all of the kinfolks got together, and that day turned into a holiday for the people."

Luciano Sánchez

Narrators: Biographical Sketches

Eduardo Valdez was born in Guadalupe on the 26th day of October, 1908. His parents were Cleto Valdez and Avelina Martínez. Though he does not remember where his father was from, his mother was born in Cebolleta, a short distance south of Guadalupe on the Río Puerco Valley. In 1927 he married Lina García. She died a few years ago, after a long illness. Eduardo Valdez, renowned for his praying ability, lived in El Bosque de Bernalillo, along the Río Grande.

Eduardo Valdez was an extremely interesting and intelligent person with a fantastic memory. Much of this is reflected in the narratives that he has provided us. His recollections vibrate with knowledge and perspicacity in a philosophical way; they are based either on personal experiences, or on legends that he inherited from his parents or grandparents. Eduardo Valdez died May 11, 1987.

Eduardo Valdez

Glossary

Regional	Standard
A	
aá	allá
abajaban	bajaban
abajito de	más allá
abajo	al plano
abajo de	debajo de
abandonao	abandonado
abujero	agujero
a case de	en casa de
aconsejalo	aconsejarlo
acostao	acostado
adelante	delante; más tarde
adentro	dentro
adivinastes	adivinaste
admirao	admirado
afusilaron	fusilaron
agarralo	agarrarlo
agarrao	agarrado
agüela (o)	abuela (o)
agüelita (o)	abuelita (o)
ai	allí
aigre	aire

Regional	Standard
ajuera	afuera
ajueritos	agujeritos
ajueros	agujeros
alabao	alabado
alargala	alargarla
almuada	almohada
alumbrao	alumbrado
amá	mamá
amás	además
ambulanza	carroza
andábanos	andábamos
andada	viaje
andao	andado
animao	animado
antonces	entonces
apá	papá
apenao	apenado
aplaneó	aplanó
apurao	apurado
arrancábanos	arrancábamos
asegún	según
asina	así
atermorizaos	atermorizados
atocante	tocante a
atrás	detrás
atrincao	atrincado
auxilialos	auxiliarlos
ayudales	ayudarles
ayudao	ayudado

B

bajao	bajado
bajo	abajo
barbaridá	barbaridad

Regional	Standard
bocabordes	carroza
bonche	montón
buscalo	buscarlo
buslándose	burlándose
buslarse	burlarse

C

Regional	Standard
cabecía	jefatura
caiba (n)	caía (n)
caida (o)	caída (o)
caidría	caería
caindo	cayendo
callao	callado
camalta	cama
cambalache	desengaño
cambiao	cambiado
caminao	caminado
cansao	cansado
cargao	cargado
carréabanos	acarréabamos
carrear	acarrear
casao	casado
case	casa
castigaos	castigados
cemeterio	cementerio
cequia	acequia
cequiecita	acequiecita
clas	clase
colgao	colgado
comigo	conmigo
condao	condado
conponiéndolo	componiéndolo
Conrao	Conrado
contemplábanos	contemplábamos
contoy	con todo

Regional	Standard
convencelo	convencerlo
correo	cartas
creiba (n)	creía (n)
creibo	creo
creyen	creen
criao	criado
criaos	criados
cruzaos	cruzados
cuidao	cuidado
cuñao	cuñado

CH

Regional	Standard
chanza	oportunidad
chequear	revisar; examinar
chupar	fumar

D

Regional	Standard
dábanos	dábamos
dale (s)	darle (s)
dao	dado
decíanos	decíamos
decile	decirle
dejates	dejaste
delante	adelante
demasana	devasana
demostrate	demostrarte
desbaratalo	desbaratarlo
desciplinaban	disciplinaban
desciplinarse	disciplinarse
desengolvieron	desenvolvieron
desmayao	desmayado
despareció	desapareció
desparecieron	desaparecieron
destendido	extendido; acostado
destendieron	extendieron
diandante	diablo
dicemos	decimos

Regional	Standard
dicía (n)	decía (n)
dijemos	decimos
dijía (n)	decía (n)
dijiendo	diciendo
dijiera (n)	dijera (n)
dijieron	dijeron
dijile	decirle
dijir	decir
dijunto	difunto
dionde	donde
diondequiera	de donde quiera
Diopoldo	Leopoldo
dites	diste
diuna	de una
donala	donarla

E

Regional	Standard
echale	echarle
echao	echado
edá	edad
eleción	elección
eletricidá	electricidad
embalsamao	embalsamado
embolao (s)	embolado (s)
empedrao	empedrado
enamoraos	enamorados
enamorates	enamoraste
encargaos	encargados
encerralas	encerrarlas
enchorraos	enchorrados
enfermedá	enfermedad
engolver	envolver
engüelvita	envueltita
enredondo	alrededor
enredor	alrededor
enseñale	enseñarle

Regional	Standard
enterrala (o)	enterrarla (o)
enterrao	enterrado
entrao	entrado
entregao	entregado
entusiasma	propuesta
envenenao	envenenado
éranos	éramos
escuchadito	calladito
escuro	oscuro
escusao	excusado
espantao	espantado
esperalo	esperarlo
espital	hospital
esposaos	esposados
esqueroso	asqueroso
estábanos	estábamos
estafeta	correos
estao	estado
estuvites	estuviste

F

fatigao	fatigado
fierro	hierro
fusilala	fusilarla

G

ganao	ganado
Gardías	Gardía
gaselín	gasolina
gaznate	cuello
golví	volví
golviera	volviera
golvieron	volvieron
golvió	volvió
Gualupe	Guadalupe

Regional	Standard
güelo	vuelo
güelta (s)	vuelta (s)
güelve (n)	vuelve (n)
güen	buen
güeno	bueno
güerfanita	huerfanita
güérfano	huérfano
güevo	huevo

H

ha	he
habelas	haberlas
habelo	haberlo
habíanos	habíamos
hablale	hablarle
hacelas	hacerlas
hacele	hacerle
hacelo	hacerlo
hacíanos	hacíamos
haiga	haya
hallao	hallado
hincaos	hincados
hogao	ahogado
hogaré	ahogaré
hogaron	ahogaron
hogó	ahogó
hombrei	hombre
horcaron	ahorcaron
huachalos	cuidarlos

I

íbanos	íbamos
impuesto	acostumbrado
injuriao	injuriado
interesao	interesado
iyendo	yendo

Regional	Standard
J	
jalla	halla
jallaba	hallaba
jallábanos	hallábamos
jallao	hallado
jallar	hallar
jallaron	hallaron
jallates	hallaste
jallé	hallé
jalló	halló
jerró	herró
jirviendo	hirviendo
jonda	honda
joyo	hoyo
jue	fue
juera	afuera; fuera
juera (n)	fuera (n)
juéranos	fuéramos
jueron	fueron
juerte	fuerte
juerza	fuerza
jui	fui
juido	huído
juimos	fuimos
juir	huir
juisque	aguardiente
juites	fuiste
juntábanos	juntábamos
juntra	junto
juquiaron	escarbaron
juyendo	huyendo
juyó	huyó
K	

Regional	Standard
L	
ladiao	ladeado
lao	lado
lazao	lazado
leelo	leerlo
leido	leído
ler	leer
leyelo	leerlo
logo	luego
lonche	almuerzo
loo	luego
LL	
llamábanos	llamábamos
llegao	llegado
llevale	llevarle
llevalo	llevarlo
llevao	llevado
M	
maiz	maíz
matalas	matarlas
matalo	matarlo
matao	matado
mentao	mentado
mercé	merced
mesmo (s)	mismo (s)
metele	meterle
mitá	mitad
mojo	moho
mojosa	mohosa
monquiando	jugando
Montaños	Montaño
montao	montado
mostrale	mostrarle

Regional	Standard
mostrao	demostrado
muche	mucho; muchas
muchichito	muchachito
muchito (s)	muchachito (s)
muncho	mucho
murre	muy

N

nadien	nadie
naguas	enaguas
naide	nadie
naiden	nadie
necesidá	necesidad
nombrábanos	nombrábamos
novedá	novedad
nuevecientos	novecientos

Ñ

ñeca	muñeca

O

ocupao	ocupado
onde	donde
ondequiera	dondequiera
oportunidá	oportunidad
ora	ahora; hora
orita	ahorita
orora	ahora mismo

P

pa	para
paá	para allá
pacá	para acá
pader	pared
pais	país
pal	para el
pallá	para allá

Regional	Standard
pan	para en
papases	papás
par	para
parao (s)	parado (s)
pasao (s)	pasado (s)
paseao	paseado
patas	pies
pecao	pecado
pedila	pedirla
pediórico	periódico
peleao	peleado
penao	penado
pene	centavo
permitemos	permitimos
pesao	pesado
platicao	platicado
podela	poderla
podíanos	podíamos
porecito	pobrecito
pos	pues
prebas	pruebas
prendele	prenderle
previniendo	preparando
privao	privado
profundidá	profundidad
publicao	publicado
pullas	púas
pus	pues

Q

Regional	Standard
quedao	quedado
quemalas	quemarlas
quemalo	quemarlo
quemao	quemado

Regional	Standard
queque	terrón
qüilta	colcha
quitásela	quitársela

R

Regional	Standard
Rafel	Rafael
rechinaido	rechinido
redamadero	derramadero
refaicionar	refleccionar
remanse	remanso
requié	choqué
resentaos	resentidos
retirao	retirado
rezábanos	rezábamos
rezao	rezado
robao	robado
roga	ruego

S

Regional	Standard
sacala	sacarla
sacale	sacarle
sacalo (s)	sacarlo (s)
sacao	sacado
sacáranos	sacáramos
sagrao	sagrado
saliéranos	saliéramos
sarpingo	cincho
seguridá	seguridad
semos	somos
sentao (s)	sentado (s)
siguimos	seguimos
silleta	silla
sociedá	sociedad
socorrelo	socorrerlo

Regional	Standard
subadero	sudadero
suidá	ciudad
suidades	ciudades

T

Regional	Standard
taá	todavía
taavía	todavía
tamién	también
tantos	cuantos
tavía	todavía
telefón	teléfono
teníanos	teníamos
tiralas	tirarlas
tiralo	tirarlo
toa	toda
toavía	todavía
tocao	tocado
toitito	toditito
tomao	tomado
tomóviles	automóviles
too (s)	todo (s)
tostao	tostado
trae	traer
traeles	traerles
traiba (n)	traía (n)
tráibanos	traíamos
traibas	traías
traido	traído
trampao	trampado
troca	camión
trojas	troj
truje	traje
trujiera (n)	trajera (n)
trujieron	trajeron

Regional		Standard
trujimos		trajimos
trujites		trajiste
trujo	.	trajo
	U	
universidá		universidad
usábanos		usábamos
usté		usted
	V	
Varisto		E(A)varisto
veiga (s)		veas
veníanos		veníamos
verdá		verdad
vía (n)		veía (n)
víanos		veíamos
vido		vio
vieja		esposa
vites		viste
vivíanos		vivíamos
voluntá		voluntad
volvites		volviste
	W	
	X	
	Y	
	Z	